An Evaluation of California's Permanent Disability Rating System

Robert T. Reville, Seth A. Seabury, Frank W. Neuhauser, John F. Burton, Jr., Michael D. Greenberg

Prepared for the
California Commission on Health and Safety and Workers' Compensation

INSTITUTE FOR CIVIL JUSTICE

The research described in this report was conducted by the RAND Institute for Civil Justice, a unit of the RAND Corporation. This research was sponsored by the California Commission on Health and Safety and Workers' Compensation.

Library of Congress Cataloging-in-Publication Data

An evaluation of California's permanent disability rating system / Robert T. Reville ... [et al.].
    p. cm.
    "MG-258."
    Includes bibliographical references.
    ISBN 0-8330-3813-3 (pbk. : alk. paper)
    1. People with disabilities—Government policy—California. 2 Disability evaluation—Law and legislation—California. I. Reville, Robert T.

HV1555.C2E83 2005
362.4'048'09794—dc22

                                          2005013897

The RAND Corporation is a nonprofit research organization providing objective analysis and effective solutions that address the challenges facing the public and private sectors around the world. RAND's publications do not necessarily reflect the opinions of its research clients and sponsors.

RAND® is a registered trademark.

Published 2005 by the RAND Corporation
1776 Main Street, P.O. Box 2138, Santa Monica, CA 90407-2138
1200 South Hayes Street, Arlington, VA 22202-5050
201 North Craig Street, Suite 202, Pittsburgh, PA 15213-1516
RAND URL: http://www.rand.org/
To order RAND documents or to obtain additional information, contact
Distribution Services: Telephone: (310) 451-7002;
Fax: (310) 451-6915; Email: order@rand.org

RAND Institute for Civil Justice

The mission of the RAND Institute for Civil Justice (ICJ), a division of the RAND Corporation, is to improve private and public decisionmaking on civil legal issues by supplying policymakers and the public with the results of objective, empirically based, analytic research. The ICJ facilitates change in the civil justice system by analyzing trends and outcomes, identifying and evaluating policy options, and bringing together representatives of different interests to debate alternative solutions to policy problems. The Institute builds on a long tradition of RAND research characterized by an interdisciplinary, empirical approach to public policy issues and rigorous standards of quality, objectivity, and independence.

ICJ research is supported by pooled grants from corporations, trade and professional associations, and individuals; by government grants and contracts; and by private foundations. The Institute disseminates its work widely to the legal, business, and research communities, and to the general public. In accordance with RAND policy, all Institute research products are subject to peer review before publication. ICJ publications do not necessarily reflect the opinions or policies of the research sponsors or of the ICJ Board of Overseers. For additional information about the RAND Institute for Civil Justice, contact:

Robert T. Reville, Director
RAND Institute for Civil Justice
1776 Main Street, P.O. Box 2138
Santa Monica, CA 90407-2138
Phone: (310) 393-0411 x6786; Fax: (310) 451-6979
E-mail: Robert_Reville@rand.org
Web: www.rand.org/icj/

ICJ Board of Overseers

California Commission on Health and Safety and Workers' Compensation

The California Commission on Health and Safety and Workers' Compensation is a joint labor-management body created by the workers' compensation reform legislation of 1993. It is charged with overseeing the health and safety and workers' compensation systems in California and recommending administrative or legislative modifications to improve their operation. The Commission works with the entire health and safety and workers' compensation community including employees, employers, labor organizations, insurers, attorneys, medical and rehabilitation providers, administrators, educators, government agencies, and members of the public to provide a more effective and efficient workers' compensation system in California.

The Commission contracts with independent research organizations for projects and studies designed to evaluate critical areas of key programs. This is done to ensure objectivity, incorporate a balance of viewpoints, and to produce the highest-quality analysis and evaluation.

Appointed by the Governor of California

Leonard C. McLeod, California Correctional Peace Officers Association, *representing labor*

Alfonso Salazar, ARS Solutions, *representing employers*

Darrel "Shorty" Thacker, Bay Counties District Council of Carpenters, *representing labor*

John C. Wilson, Schools Excess Liability Fund, *representing employers*

Appointed by the Speaker of the California Assembly

Allen Davenport, Service Employees International Union California State Council, *representing labor*

Robert B. Steinberg, Law Offices of Rose, Klein and Marias, *representing employers*

Appointed by the Senate Rules Committee

Kristen Schwenkmeyer, Gordon and Schwenkmeyer, *representing employers*

Angie Wei, California Labor Federation, AFL-CIO, *representing labor*

Executive Officer

Christine Baker

Preface

In 1996, the California Commission on Health and Safety and Workers' Compensation (CHSWC) commissioned RAND to begin an extensive review of the workers' compensation permanent partial disability (PPD) system in California. As part of that evaluation, ICJ studied the adequacy of PPD benefits for injured workers at private, insured firms (employers that purchase workers' compensation insurance from private insurance carriers) (Peterson, Reville, and Stern 1997) and at private, self-insured firms (employers that cover the costs of compensation for employees' injuries out of their own pockets) (Reville et al., 2001c). ICJ has also examined the workers' compensation court system (Pace et al., 2003) and medical fee schedules (Wynn et al., 2003).

With this study, we report the final results of our evaluation of how well the California PPD system assesses permanent disabilities from workplace injuries and assigns benefits to injured workers. This monograph provides further documentation on and discussion of the results reported in an ICJ interim briefing on California's permanent disability rating schedule (Reville, Seabury, and Neuhauser, 2003). The results reported in the interim briefing provided policymakers with valuable information about the strengths and weaknesses of the California disability rating system and offered empirical evidence to inform an ongoing debate over the PPD system that previously had relied on anecdotal evidence.

The research reported here should help to guide the implementation of recent reforms to the California workers' compensation system. In addition, we hope that the disability rating methods discussed in this report will inform an ongoing evaluation of California's PPD system that will ultimately lead to greater equity in benefits for injured workers and minimize unnecessary disputes between injured workers and their employers.

This monograph should be of interest to policymakers, stakeholders, and others interested in the efficacy and equity of the delivery of permanent disability benefits to workers' compensation recipients. While the focus of this report is on workers' compensation in California, many findings reported here should have broader applications to systems in other U.S. states and the Canadian provinces.

Contents

Figures

Tables

Summary

When workers suffer a permanently disabling injury at the workplace, they are usually eligible to receive workers' compensation benefits. A defining characteristic of permanent partial disability (PPD) benefits in California and other states is that more-severely injured workers are entitled to higher benefits than less-severely injured workers. This characteristic of PPD benefits necessitates a system for ranking the severity of various impairments for both single parts of the body and across different body parts. This ranking, called the *permanent disability rating,* is used to distribute PPD benefits to workers with various types of impairments. In California, injured workers with higher disability ratings are entitled to more benefits than those with lower ratings.

The disability rating process sparks controversy in every state, but nowhere has it been more controversial than in California. California has historically relied on its own system for measuring disability, a system that has been criticized by many observers as being inconsistent, prone to promote disputes, and conducive to fraud. In this report, we discuss the criteria that are used to evaluate different types of injury, and the system for delivering benefits in California, and compare those criteria to the criteria used in other jurisdictions. This discussion provides a useful framework for thinking about the various principles upon which the equity and efficacy of California's PPD benefits delivery system can be judged. We then provide a systematic empirical evaluation of California's permanent disability ratings system. We examine the extent to which workers with higher ratings experience higher earnings losses, and the extent to which workers with similar ratings for impairments in different parts of the body suffer similar earnings losses. In addition, we study how other factors, such as early return to work,[1] impact losses, and we examine the consistency of different physicians' assessments of the same impairment.

---

[1] *Return to work* is a term used by participants in the workers' compensation system to describe various aspects of employment following injury. Sometimes also called the *return to work rate,* the term usually refers to the amount of time between an injury and the first day of return to work. More generally, the term refers to both return to work rates for injured employees and other characteristics of post-injury employment, such as retention and subsequent employment. In this report, "return to work" implies the latter, more general definition.

Background on the Disability Ratings Controversy in California

Workers' compensation must include a means for assigning benefits—i.e., a structured system for converting the medical evaluation of a permanent impairment from a workplace injury into a quantitative measure of the severity of the injured worker's disability. In California, the PPD rating system converts the quantitative measure (the *disability rating*) into a benefit amount based on the worker's pre-injury wage. PPD benefits are paid to workers who have injuries that are serious enough to have permanent consequences but are not serious enough to be totally disabling. Higher ratings translate into higher benefits, reflecting the fact that one would expect more-serious injuries to have a more disabling effect on a person's ability to work.

Historically, California's approach to assigning benefits has differed markedly from that used by most other states, and critics blame that approach for many of the ills of the state's workers' compensation system. In 1996, the California Commission on Health and Safety and Workers' Compensation (CHSWC) commissioned the RAND Corporation to begin an extensive review of PPD benefits in California; the study described in this report is one of five that RAND eventually completed. In late 2003, we delivered to CHSWC an interim report on our findings from this study. The interim report helped to inform the policy debates that ultimately resulted in Senate Bill (SB) 899, a 2004 bill that reformed many aspects of the state's workers' compensation system, including the permanent disability rating system. This report provides more formal documentation of our evaluation of the system *pre*-reform and additional discussion of potential issues to be considered within the post-reform system.

The California permanent disability system attempted to produce a measure of disability that combined both severity of an impairment and the effect of the impairment on work. The disability ratings were based on a variety of objective and subjective criteria. The reliance on subjective criteria to measure disability was the most controversial feature of the California system and what most distinguished it from the systems used in other states. Supporters of the system contended that California's unique approach to compensating disabilities better targeted benefits to workers, and that some disabilities, while real, cannot be objectively measured using medical criteria. Critics of the system countered that the use of these criteria led to excessive PPD claiming and an inappropriate distribution of benefits.

Our approach cannot test the merits of considering subjective factors, because we cannot separately identify disability ratings that do or do not include a subjective component. Likewise, because we have data on only ratings using the California system, we cannot say whether the system performed any better or any worse than any other state's system. Nevertheless, we are able to address some of the criticisms that have been directed at the old system and explore the potential for empirical data on earnings loss to improve permanent disability ratings.

Research Questions and Approach

As requested by CHSWC, RAND undertook a sweeping evaluation of the PPD rating system. The study largely focused on the following questions:

- Did the PPD system ensure that the highest ratings (and therefore the most benefits) go to the most severely impaired individuals?
- Did individuals with different types of impairments but similar disability severity receive similar ratings?
- Would different physicians examining the same impairment provide assessments that lead to similar ratings?
- Were the inconsistencies in physician ratings substantial enough to provide parties with incentives to litigate (given the adversarial nature of the system)?

To address these questions, RAND analyzed data on almost 350,000 PPD claims in California, from the sample of cases with an injury date between January 1, 1991, and April 1, 1997, that were rated by the state's Disability Evaluation Unit (DEU). Because several years of post-injury earnings must be observed to estimate earnings losses, injuries occurring after April 1, 1997, were not used. We were able to match most (more than 69 percent) of the injured workers in this sample to administrative data on wages from the Employment Development Department (EDD). Thus, we were able to create a database that includes the type of impairment, disability rating, and the estimated earnings losses for 241,685 PPD claimants in California.[2]

Using these data, we can compare the disability ratings produced by the DEU with the observed earnings outcomes. Earnings-loss estimates provide a direct measure of how a permanent disability affects an individual's ability to compete in the labor market. This measure provides the empirical basis that had previously been lacking to evaluate the ranking of impairments. By comparing the disability ratings and earnings losses of injured workers in California, we can directly assess the extent to which the PPD rating system provides injured workers with appropriate compensation.

Did Workers Receive Benefits Appropriate to Their Injuries?

Our analysis showed that, on average, the pre–SB 899 California rating system appeared to function reasonably well in terms of targeting higher PPD benefits to

---

[2] The methodology for estimating earnings losses for disabled workers is the same as that used in past studies, including Peterson et al. (1997), Reville (1999), and Reville et al. (2001c).

workers with higher proportional losses. This finding is illustrated in Figure S.1, which shows the average three-year (12 quarters) cumulative proportional earnings losses for those cases with disability ratings of 1–10 percent, 11–20 percent, and so forth, up to ratings of 91–100 percent. The figure includes two stages of the disability rating, the unadjusted *standard rating* and the *final rating*.[3] If the disability rating system targets higher benefits effectively to more-severely injured workers, then we would expect to see the average earnings losses increase as we move from left to right in Figure S.1. This is clearly the case; the average proportional losses for cases with a rating of 1–10 percent are about 5 percent, while the losses for those with a rating of 91–100 percent are more than 60 percent. This positive association holds for almost every rating category, allowing us to conclude that, on average, California's injured workers who have more-severe impairments appear to receive higher PPD benefits.

The targeting of higher benefits to the more-severe impairments is only one objective of the rating schedule; another is to ensure that the ratings are distributed equitably for impairments to different parts of the body. In theory, the rating system

Figure S.1
Three-Year Cumulative Proportional Earnings Losses by Disability Rating Group

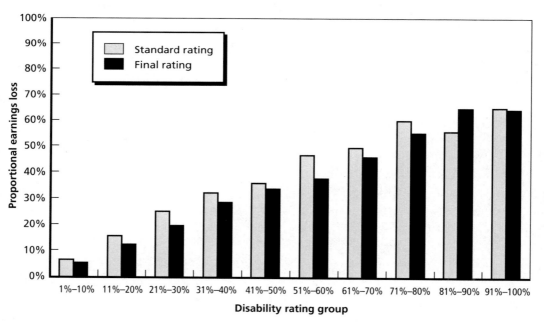

---

[3] The standard rating is based solely on physician evaluation of disability severity (using objective and subjective factors), while the final rating incorporates additional adjustments for age and occupation.

is supposed to incorporate *all* the medical information that is relevant for determining the severity of an impairment, suggesting that, for example, an impairment to the back and an impairment to the shoulder that have the same impact on an individual's ability to compete in the labor market should receive the same rating. In this report, we document that the overall positive relationship between earnings losses and disability ratings masks considerable differences in the distribution of benefits across impairments to different body parts.

Past work has already demonstrated substantial inequities among the ratings assigned to different upper-extremity impairments (Reville et al., 2002a). Figure S.2 extends the analysis to consider four major impairment categories—shoulder, knee, back, and loss of grasping power.[4] Two key results should be noted from this analysis. The proportional earnings losses for every type of impairment increase with the increase in the disability rating. This finding reflects the fact that the system targets disability benefits appropriately to more-severe impairments on average *within a*

Figure S.2
Three-Year Losses by Disability Rating Category by Injury Type

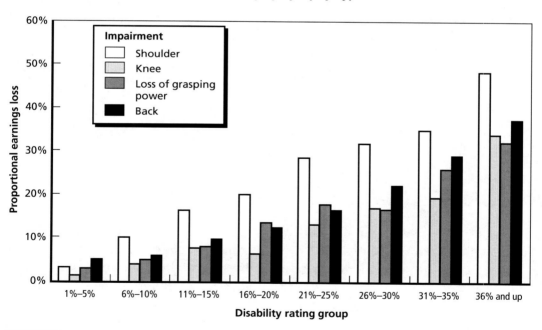

---

[4] Because the number of observations grows small for individual rating categories for ratings above 35 percent, in Figure S.2 we present finer groups of lower-rated claims and lump together the higher-rated claims.

given body part. However, it is also apparent that there are clear disparities among the observed proportional earnings losses for different impairments that are given similar ratings.

The overall positive relationship between earnings losses and disability ratings masks considerable differences in the distribution of benefits across impairments to different body parts. In the lowest disability-rating group (ratings of 1–5 percent), back injuries have the highest estimated losses, about 4.6 percent, while knee injuries have the lowest, about 0.9 percent. For all other rating groups, however, shoulder injuries have substantially higher proportional earnings losses than all other types of injury. Knee injuries have the lowest earnings losses on average, although the loss of grasping power seems to have the lowest percentage of losses for the highest rating category. These disparities are even more pronounced if we consider psychiatric impairments (not illustrated here). All psychiatric claims, regardless of rating, have substantial earnings losses, exceeding 38 percent on average. Additionally, even low-rated psychiatric claims have a higher percentage of losses than all but the highest-rated claims for the other impairment types.

These results provide a striking illustration of the impact of a lack of empirical bases for disability rating schedules. It is usually possible to show that, between two individuals with the same impairment, one impairment is more severe than the other. This is why, within impairment type, every rating group has higher proportional wage losses than the next-lowest rating group. However, it is far more difficult to compare severity across impairments to different body parts. Moreover, equally severe impairments (as measured by the disability rating) to different body parts each impact earnings differently. Using wage losses to evaluate impairment severity allows us to provide a common standard of comparison across impairment types.

Ability to Return to Work Impacts Long-Term Earnings

While California's disability rating system incorporates a number of important factors that might indicate an individual's earnings capacity, one factor that it does not consider in rating a disability is the observed return to work by an individual. Return to work, particularly return to the at-injury employer, is an important factor because it is a strong predictor of the long-term economic outcomes of disabled workers. Despite this fact, an injured worker in California receives the same compensation whether or not he or she returns to work. Injured workers who continue at the at-injury employer may actually receive benefits that exceed their earnings losses after tax considerations are taken into account, at least for some period of time after the date of injury.

Figure S.3 displays the estimated three-year proportional earnings losses for permanently disabled workers in California by their disability rating. The lighter gray bars show the average proportional losses for all disabled workers, whether or not they are observed returning to work (the "Unconditional" losses). The darker gray bars represent the average three-year losses of workers who are observed at the at-injury employer four quarters (one year) after the date of injury. The black bars represent the average three-year losses for workers who are observed working eight quarters (two years) after the date of injury.

Figure S.3 makes it clear that, at every level of severity, workers who return to the at-injury employer experience much lower long-term proportional earnings losses than those who do not. While the differences in earnings losses among workers with very low disability ratings (those between 1 percent and 10 percent) are very small, workers with medium or severe disabilities have much lower earnings losses if they return to the at-injury employer. For example, for disabled workers with a disability rating of 11–20 percent, the overall proportional losses are approximately 12 percent, but the overall proportional losses are just 8 percent for workers with the same disability ratings who are observed at the at-injury employer one year after injury and 6 percent for workers observed at the at-injury employer two years after injury. For more severe disabilities, such as those with ratings of 41–50 percent, the overall

Figure S.3
Three-Year Proportional Earnings Losses for Injured Workers in California by Disability Rating Group and Return-to-Work Status

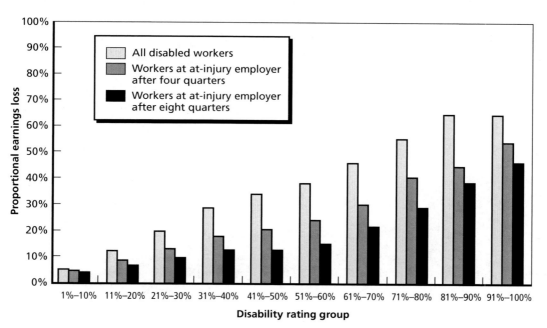

losses are approximately 34 percent, compared with losses of 20 percent for those working at the at-injury employer one year after injury and just 13 percent for those working at the at-injury employer two years after injury. Note that we do not indicate whether the worker is employed full time, so even modified work might have a positive impact on long-term earnings outcomes.

In this report, we discuss how other states use *two-tier benefit* systems to factor in return to work when assigning PPD benefits. Two-tier systems, which provide relatively lower benefits to workers who receive a legitimate employment offer from the at-injury employer and higher benefits to those who do not, can boost labor market participation for disabled workers by providing both employers and workers with incentives to offer and accept, respectively, modified employment opportunities at the at-injury employer. Two-tier systems have the potential to improve the equity of disability benefits while also improving the earnings and employment of disabled workers.

Large Inconsistencies in Disability Ratings by Physicians

The reliance on subjective factors in the California rating system has led to numerous accusations that disability ratings are assigned inconsistently in the state. An inconsistent disability rating system is one in which two physicians can evaluate the same injured individual and produce different disability ratings. If a rating system involves a substantial degree of subjectivity, then it would stand to reason that there is substantial room for variation among physicians' assessments, potentially leading to inconsistency in the ratings.

To study this issue, we can take advantage of the fact that the DEU data include three kinds of ratings: applicant, defense, and summary. An *applicant rating* is a rating based on the medical report of a physician hired by the applicant (the injured worker); similarly, a *defense rating* is based on the medical report of a physician hired by the defense (the "payer," which is either the employer or the employer's insurer). *Summary ratings* are typically based on a report by a randomly assigned "qualified medical examiner" or an "agreed medical evaluator" selected by both parties, who can plausibly be considered neutral.

As stated earlier, disability benefits increase with the increase in ratings, so a physician's report that is favorable to the applicant will lead to higher benefits, whereas a physician's report that is favorable to the defense will lead to lower benefits. Because the physicians that produce summary ratings can plausibly be considered to be neutral, their ratings should not lead to systematically higher or lower ratings than the "true" or "correct" rating.[5] By examining applicant, defense, and summary reports *for the same injury*, we can extract some information on the extent to which ratings in the California system differ due to variability in physician evaluations. Given that disability *raters* (state employees charged with converting physician medical reports into actual ratings), like summary physicians, can plausibly be considered neutral, any systematic differences between the ratings by physician type should be independent of rater inconsistency (in other words, the error by raters can be assumed to have a mean of zero).

We find clear support for our initial hypothesis that the applicant rating on average is greater than the summary rating, which in turn is greater on average than the defense rating. Cases with multiple ratings tend to involve more-severe disabilities on average; they have an average summary rating of 30.43. The average applicant rating is 37.07, 6.63 percentage points higher than the summary rating (a difference of about 22 percent). The average defense rating is 28.29, which is 2.15 percentage points (or 7 percent) lower than the summary rating. Both sets of differences are statistically significant.

While our results suggest that there are large differences in evaluations by different physicians for the same case, it is not clear the extent to which this discrepancy in evaluations is driven by the old, pre–SB 899 California rating system. For example, we examined the regional differences in ratings and found that the inconsistency in ratings is considerably higher in Southern California than in the Central Coast region or Northern California. In Southern California, for cases with all three types of ratings (applicant, defense, and summary), the average summary rating is 31.86; the average applicant rating is 7.92 points (25 percent) higher than the summary rating; and the average defense rating is 3.72 points (12 percent) lower than the summary rating. In the Central Coast region, the applicant rating is just 11 percent higher than the summary rating on average, and the defense rating is just 3 percent lower than the summary rating, with the latter difference being statistically indistinguishable from zero. The difference between applicant and defense ratings in Northern California is 20 percent, comparable to that in Southern California. In comparison, the difference between the defense and summary ratings is negligible in Northern California.

While we cannot say how much of the discrepancy between physicians' assessments is attributable or not attributable to the rating system, it appears that other factors (e.g., the relative litigiousness by region of parties in a workers' compensation claim) may be just as important. Whatever its root cause, the differences in disability ratings can have a substantial impact on the disability benefits assigned to injured workers. For example, with three different ratings for the same injury, a worker

---

[5] It is important to note that our assumptions about physicians (or raters, for that matter) may not hold for any particular individual. We simply argue that these relationships should hold *on average*.

might receive $47,000 with the applicant rating, $37,000 with the summary rating, and $33,000 with the defense rating. These differences are substantial for injured workers, as well as for payers, and may fuel disputes and litigation.

Changes to the Permanent Disability Rating System in California

In the post–SB 899 system, reforms have been adopted that could affect many of the results presented in this report. One key change is that the new approach to rating permanent disability in California abandons the old rating schedule and adopts the "objective" criteria used by the *AMA Guides to the Evaluation of Permanent Impairment* (referred to as the *AMA Guides)* (American Medical Association, 2000). However, the California legislature also called for disability ratings to reflect the estimated wage losses of injured workers based on the nature of the workers' impairments. Our results suggest that reordering the ratings to be consistent with average proportional losses for a particular impairment has the potential to improve equity in the system. However, because we have no data linking earnings losses to *AMA Guides* ratings, it is impossible to predict what the outcome of this reform will be.

A greater reliance on the use of objective factors could lead to reductions in the extent of inconsistency in physicians' assessments, if ratings under the *AMA Guides* truly are more objective. However, the differences across the three regions of the state lead to some questions about the extent to which the rating system is the root cause of inconsistencies between physicians' assessments. Another reform in SB 899 is the adoption of a two-tier system, which provides higher benefits to workers who do not receive an offer of post-injury employment when they are medically able to return to work. This system could provide employers with incentives to find appropriate employment for injured workers.

Acknowledgments

We are grateful to the members of the California Commission on Health and Safety and Workers' Compensation for their support of this research. We would like to thank Christine Baker, the Executive Director of the Commission, for providing valuable input and for helping to ensure that this research both informed, and was informed by, the workers' compensation community. We would also like to thank Irina Nemirovsky at the Commission for her help and support.

We appreciate the support of numerous people in the California Department of Labor and Department of Industrial Relations in acquiring the data for this project. In particular, we would like to thank Rich Kilthau of the Employment Development Department and Blair Megowan of the Disability Evaluation Unit.

Many colleagues provided valuable input into this project. Craig Martin (RAND) and Sue Polich (RAND) provided excellent programming support throughout this project. Jay Bhattacharya (Stanford University), Les Boden (Boston University), David Studdert (Harvard University), and Eric Talley (University of Southern California and RAND) all provided helpful comments. Soeren Mattke (RAND) and Jeff Biddle (Michigan State University) provided excellent comments, criticism, and suggestions during the review process for this report.

Within RAND, we would like to thank Karen Alkofer, Nancy Good, Joanna Nelsen, and Isabel Sardou for their administrative assistance during this project. The report benefited from excellent comments from Laura Zakaras and Shelley Wiseman and editing by Nancy DelFavero. Carole Gresenz provided valuable input to the report.

Any errors or omissions are the sole responsibility of the authors.

Acronyms

AB	Assembly Bill
ADL	activity of daily living
AMA	American Medical Association
AWL	actual wage loss
C&R	compromise and release
CHSWC	California Commission on Health and Safety and Workers' Compensation
DCBS	Oregon Department of Consumer and Business Services
DEU	(California) Disability Evaluation Unit
EDD	(California) Employment Development Department
FL	functional limitation
IMC	California Industrial Medical Council
IQR	inter-quartile range
LAWL	limited actual wage loss
LCNA	loss of capacity for nonwork activities
LEC	loss of earning capacity
MMI	maximum medical improvement
NCCI	National Council on Compensation Insurance
ND	nonwork disability
NEL	noneconomic loss
PCR	prevention, compensation, and rehabilitation
PDRS	Permanent Disability Rating System
PI	permanent impairment
PPD	permanent partial disability

PPI	"pure" permanent impairment
PTHS	post-traumatic head syndrome
SB	Senate Bill
TTD	temporary total disability
UI	unemployment insurance
WCIRB	California Workers' Compensation Insurance Rating Bureau
WD	work disability
WL	wage loss
WLDI	Work Loss Data Institute

CHAPTER ONE

Introduction

Historically, the California workers' compensation system has employed a unique approach to rating permanent partial disabilities (PPDs) for the purpose of determining benefits for injured workers.[1] Depending on the injury, information on either functional limitation or impairment might be used for these ratings, and sometimes both have been used. Benefits are then determined based on the perceived effect of that specific impairment or limitation on the individual's ability to compete in the labor market. Proponents of the California system have argued that it has been among the most ambitious and comprehensive schemes in the country for compensating individuals for the effects of disability. Critics of the California system have countered that the system has been cumbersome, has done a poor job of targeting benefits, and has provided incentives for litigation.

By 2004, the state's workers' compensation system was associated with the highest employer costs in the nation despite evidence indicating that the state's injured workers were not being adequately compensated. This situation led to considerable impetus for workers' compensation reform, with a particular focus on the evaluation and compensation of permanent disabilities. This reform effort led to a sweeping overhaul of the California permanent partial disability rating system. In this chapter, we briefly describe the problems and controversies associated with the California PPD rating system, discuss our approach to evaluating the effectiveness of the system with respect to these criticisms, and summarize some of the reforms that have been enacted.

---

[1] In talking about permanent *partial* disabilities, we are making an implicit distinction between those disabilities and permanent *total* disabilities. Permanent total disabilities are compensated differently than permanent partial disabilities, and our discussion in this report is relevant only for the latter. But, for simplicity's sake, we frequently use the terms permanent disability and permanent partial disability interchangeably.

Issues That Motivated Reform

High Costs

The recent workers' compensation reforms in California are in response to the significantly increasing costs of the system. A state-by-state comparison of data on average workers' compensation insurance premium rates for 2002 per $100 of payroll (weighted to control for industrial differences across states) by the Oregon Department of Consumer and Business Services (DCBS) showed that California had the highest average premium rates in the country (Reinke and Manley, 2003). Insured employers in California paid $5.23 per $100 of payroll for their workers' compensation insurance, more than 16 percent more than the $4.50 paid by employers in Florida, which had the second-highest average rates. Not only was California the only state with a rate that exceeded $5 per $100 of payroll, Florida was the only other state with a rate exceeding $4, and just seven states had rates of $3 or higher. Arizona had an average rate of $1.63 per $100 of payroll, less than one-third the average rate in California.

The DCBS comparison was based on California rates as of January 1, 2002. After that date, California rates rose rapidly. The California Workers' Compensation Insurance Rating Bureau (WCIRB) estimated average rates for the third quarter of 2003 at $6.33 per $100 of payroll. These dollar figures illustrate that the workers' compensation system imposes severe costs on employers in California, more so than any other state.

Poor Labor Market Outcomes for Injured Workers

Regrettably, the higher costs paid by California employers do not necessarily result in better economic outcomes for California's injured workers, according to research by RAND (Boden, Reville, and Biddle, 2005). That study finds that while average benefits paid for PPD are highest in California, California's injured workers are far more likely to be out of work after their injuries, and in the long run, the benefits to workers cannot compensate the resulting lower earnings. Specifically, Californians with PPD claims lose more than 25 percent of the earnings they would have received from employment over the ten years after injury. In contrast, workers in Washington and Oregon lose less than 20 percent of their earnings. These results are driven by poor *return to work*[2] in California as compared with return to work in other states.

When lower return to work rates and higher earnings losses in California are taken into account, the fraction of lost wages replaced by benefits (the most widely

---

[2] *Return to work* is a term used by participants in the workers' compensation system to describe various aspects of employment following injury. Sometimes also called the *return to work rate,* the term usually refers to the amount of time between an injury and the first day of return to work. More generally, the term refers to both return to work rates for injured employees and other characteristics of post-injury employment, such as retention and subsequent employment. In this report, "return to work" implies the latter, more general definition.

accepted measure of benefit adequacy) is lower in California than in Washington, Oregon, and New Mexico—all of which are lower-cost states. The outcomes for injured workers in California and four comparison states (New Mexico, Oregon, Washington, and Wisconsin) are presented in Table 1.1.

RAND studies are not the only ones to highlight the poor return-to-work outcomes in California. A study by the Work Loss Data Institute (WLDI, 2003) ranks states by the duration of temporary total disability (TTD) benefits (with lower rankings indicating more time out of work) and ranks California 42nd out of 44 jurisdictions.

These results highlight the fundamental problem with the California workers' compensation system—it has been failing both employers and injured workers. This problem has left policymakers in California with a considerable challenge: finding ways to reduce the cost of workers' compensation for employers while improving the long-term economic prospects of California's injured workers.

High Rates of Litigation
One factor driving higher costs in California has been the adversarial nature of the workers' compensation system. Boden, Reville, and Biddle (2005) show that in California at least 30 percent of workers with eight or more days out of work eventually hire an attorney to represent them—twice the percentage as in Oregon, the state with the next-highest percentage of workers who hire attorneys. While attorneys provide valuable services to injured workers, workers' compensation is an administrative system that was intended to provide benefits to injured workers expeditiously while reducing litigation. These results suggest that the system has failed to deliver benefits in this manner.

The California system has long been considered one of the country's most litigious. This characteristic of the system is problematic because litigation is costly, and because it can place employers and injured workers at odds with each other. Conflict between an injured worker and his or her employer is likely to reduce the chance that the injured worker returns to the at-injury employer, damaging the worker's long-

Table 1.1
Ten-Year Earnings Losses and Replacement Rates for PPD Claimants in California and Four Comparison States

	California	Washington	New Mexico	Wisconsin	Oregon
Ten-year losses ($)	58,606	41,220	34,552	49,477	35,727
Potential earnings ($)	229,472	250,251	167,106	222,055	194,923
Total benefits ($)	21,822	16,734	15,824	14,452	13,914
Proportional wage loss	25.5%	16.5%	20.7%	22.3%	18.3%
Before-tax replacement of lost wages	37.2%	40.6%	45.8%	29.2%	38.9%

term economic prospects. One of the express goals of workers' compensation is to minimize disputes between injured workers and their employers, so the persistent contentiousness of the California system is clearly a matter of concern.

Permanent Partial Disability and Recent Reforms

Permanent partial disability benefits are paid to workers who have injuries that are serious enough to have permanent consequences but that are not serious enough to be totally disabling. PPD benefits are not only the most expensive but also the most controversial and complex type of workers' compensation indemnity (i.e., cash) benefits. One reason for the complexity is the fact that the criteria and procedures for and relative share of PPD benefits vary widely among states.

Much of the controversy surrounding PPD in California has focused on the rating schedule. The *rating schedule* is used to convert the medical evaluation of an impairment into a quantitative measure of the severity of the disability. This measure, the *disability rating*, is then converted into a benefit amount based on the pre-injury wage. Higher ratings translate into higher benefits, reflecting the fact that one would expect more serious injuries to have a more disabling effect on a person's ability to work.

Critics of the PPD system have often pointed to the rating system as driving litigation in California. As we discuss later in detail, the most controversial feature of the California system is its reliance on "subjective" criteria and work restrictions to measure disability. Detractors argue that the use of these criteria has led to excessive PPD claiming and an inappropriate distribution of benefits. Supporters of the system contend that California's unique approach to compensating disability better targets benefits to workers, and that some disabilities, while real, cannot be objectively measured using medical criteria alone.

Study Purpose and Approach

In 1996, the California Commission on Health and Safety and Workers' Compensation (CHSWC) commissioned RAND to begin an extensive review of the PPD system in California. This report is the last of five reports on the subject.[3] Its focus is the evaluation of the rating system used to assess the extent of disability and to assign benefits. We examined data on disability ratings and earnings losses of injured workers under the system that existed prior to recent legislation—Senate Bill (SB) 899,

---

[3] The other four reports are Peterson et al. (1997), Reville et al. (2001b), Reville et al. (2001c), and Reville et al. (2003).

the California Workers' Compensation Reform Act (effective April 19, 2004), which called for substantial changes in the rating system—in an attempt to answer a number of questions:

- Did the PPD system ensure that the highest ratings (and therefore the most benefits) go to the most severely impaired individuals?
- Did individuals with different types of impairments but similar disability severity receive similar ratings?
- Would different physicians examining the same impairment provide assessments that lead to similar ratings?
- Were the inconsistencies in physician ratings substantial enough to provide parties with incentives to litigate (given the adversarial nature of the system)?

By addressing these questions we hoped to (1) provide valuable information to policymakers about the performance of the rating schedule and (2) offer an empirically based set of guidelines for measuring the consequences of a permanently disabling workplace injury, which might ultimately be used as a roadmap for revising the PPD rating schedule. Ultimately, SB 899 revised the schedule, and the analyses described in this report have helped to shape the new system that has been adopted.

To answer these questions, we combined administrative data on disability ratings and earnings for PPD claimants in California from 1991 to 1997. If disability ratings are intended to compensate for an individual's lost ability to compete in the labor market, then the earnings losses experienced by injured workers should serve as an independent measure of impairment. Thus, we can evaluate the rating system by determining whether individuals with higher earnings losses also receive higher ratings. Additionally, we can examine whether individuals with similar observable impairment characteristics also have similar earnings losses. These methods are described in greater detail in Chapter Five.

Impact of Study Findings

There are a number of interesting findings from this study. First, the California PPD rating system (before the recent reform legislation) appeared to target benefits appropriately to the most seriously impaired workers on average. However, there were large disparities in the earnings losses suffered by workers with similarly rated impairments in different parts of the body. Additionally, the study results question the validity of the age-adjustment factor that awards older workers higher ratings than younger workers for the same injuries. We also examine the use of return to work as an indicator of long-term earnings losses and describe policies used in other states to incorporate return to work into the delivery of disability benefits. Finally, we found considerable variation in ratings based on different physician's reports, variation that may have provided incentives to litigate.

Preliminary results from this study were first made available in an interim documented briefing (Reville et al., 2003) on permanent disability published in December 2003 in the midst of the legislative debate leading up to SB 899. Ultimately, the results from that earlier document were cited in the changes that SB 899 introduced into the system for rating permanent disabilities. The new law abandons the use of both subjective criteria and work restrictions in a permanent disability rating. Instead, the SB 899 rating is to be based on the criteria used in the American Medical Association (AMA) *Guides to the Evaluation of Permanent Impairment* (American Medical Association, 2000; hereafter referred to as the *AMA Guides*), which rely primarily on "objective" medical evidence of disability. However, the California legislature elected to adopt a modification to the *AMA Guides* that is designed to reflect the estimated wage losses of injured workers based on the nature of their impairment. Specifically, the legislation reads:

Section 4660 of the Labor Code is amended to read:

4660. (a) In determining the percentages of permanent disability, account shall be taken of the nature of the physical injury or disfigurement, the occupation of the injured employee, and his or her age at the time of the injury, consideration being given to an employee's diminished future earning capacity.

(b) (1) For purposes of this section, the "nature of the physical injury or disfigurement" shall incorporate the descriptions and measurements of physical impairments and the corresponding percentages of impairments published in the American Medical Association (AMA) *Guides to the Evaluation of Permanent Impairment* (5th Edition).

(2) For purposes of this section, an employee's diminished future earning capacity shall be a numeric formula based on empirical data and findings that aggregate the average percentage of long-term loss of income resulting from each type of injury for similarly situated employees. The administrative director shall formulate the adjusted rating schedule based on empirical data and findings from the *Evaluation of California's Permanent Disability Rating Schedule, Interim Report* (December 2003), prepared by the RAND Institute for Civil Justice, and upon data from additional empirical studies.

The last provision makes California the first state to base the assignment of disability benefits on empirical evidence about the earnings losses attributable to different impairments. The empirical findings in this report elaborate upon and complement those of the interim report cited in the legislation.

Organization of This Report

Chapter Two defines some key terms and concepts that are useful in discussing PPD. In particular, we define the criteria under which PPD benefits are and can be evaluated. Past RAND studies focused primarily on one of those criteria: the adequacy of benefits. This study focuses more on two other criteria: equity and delivery system efficiency. As discussed in that chapter, a full evaluation of PPD requires an examination of these criteria and others.

In Chapter Three, we discuss in greater detail California's method of rating permanent disabilities. The rating schedule is the focus of our empirical analysis, so Chapter Four describes what that schedule is, how it has evolved over time, and how it differs from the rating schedules of other states. In Chapter Four, we also provide a detailed examination of an important issue in disability evaluation: the assessment of chronic pain. We study how the *AMA Guides* assess pain, and we compare these methods to the standards used in the California system.

Chapter Five presents our empirical evaluation of the California rating schedule. We begin by analyzing the ability of the rating schedule to target disability benefits to more disabled workers—that is, workers with worse economic outcomes. This analysis builds on Reville et al. (2002a), which focused on upper extremity musculoskeletal injuries. In Chapter Five, we extend the 2002 analysis to a much more representative set of injuries in the California system, allowing us to determine whether the same inequities found for upper-extremity injuries are present throughout the system for other injuries.

In Chapter Six, we discuss our study of the use of other adjustments for disability ratings (and benefits) in the California workers' compensation system. We study the earnings losses of PPD claimants by age and examine whether or not older workers suffer higher earnings losses, as is implied by the age adjustment. In addition, we examine earnings losses based on whether or not a worker returns to work, which is a factor that has not been used to inform ratings in California but is in other states and will be under SB 899.

In Chapter Seven, we use claims that were evaluated by two different physicians to study the consistency of disability ratings. Chapter Eight concludes with key findings and issues and questions related to possible additional reform. The appendices offer further details on permanent disability ratings in California.

CHAPTER TWO

A Framework for Analyzing Permanent Partial Disability

The purpose of this chapter is to provide a framework for thinking about the various issues involved with compensating workers for PPD. We begin with an introduction to the basic concepts that are central to understanding the important features of PPD benefits, including a description of the permanent consequences of injuries and diseases. We then examine the policy issues that every jurisdiction must address (explicitly or implicitly) in designing a system of PPD benefits. Appendix A describes the various operational approaches adopted by the states to compensate permanent disability.

Basic Concepts and Terminology

States differ significantly in their approach to compensating permanent disabilities, such as the operational approach used to provide PPD benefits. Furthermore, even among jurisdictions using the same operational procedures, the terminology used to describe the criteria for determining benefits may differ. Thus, a common set of terms is a practical necessity for effective inter-jurisdictional comparisons regarding PPD benefits.

The Three Time Periods: Pre-Injury, Temporary Disability, and Permanent Disability

Figure 2.1 displays the three distinct time periods that are pertinent in compensating a worker with an injury or disease serious enough to result in PPD benefits. The employee's average wage in the *pre-injury period* is used in calculating the cash benefits paid by the workers' compensation program. The consequences of a work-related injury or disease can be categorized as temporary or permanent, a distinction that has an important bearing on the types of benefits provided under workers' compensation. The *temporary disability period* refers to the period of time from the onset of the injury or disease until the date when maximum medical improvement (MMI) is reached; the *permanent disability period* refers to the period following MMI. In California, the date when the injury is considered "permanent and stationary" corresponds to the date of MMI, as that term is used in most jurisdictions. In this report, we use permanent and stationary and MMI interchangeably.

Permanent Consequences of Disability

Most workers injured on the job fully recover by the date of MMI and thus sustain no permanent consequences from their injury. For those workers with relatively serious injuries, any of several permanent consequences is possible. There may be a persistence of pain and suffering and/or a continuing need for medical care and rehabilitation. Other permanent consequences, shown in Figure 2.2, are of particular interest for this study, because they are the focus of most of the debate concerning the optimal design of PPD benefits provisions in a workers' compensation program.

Figure 2.1
The Three Time Periods of a Workers' Compensation Case When an Injury Has Permanent Consequences

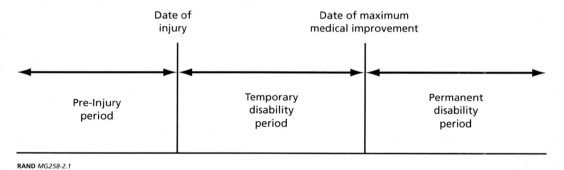

RAND *MG258-2.1*

Figure 2.2
Permanent Consequences of an Injury or Disease

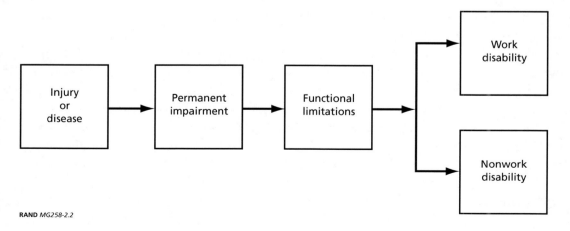

RAND *MG258-2.2*

A *permanent impairment* (PI) is any anatomic or functional abnormality or loss that remains after MMI has been achieved. Amputated limbs or enervated muscles are examples of permanent impairments. The impairment probably causes the worker to experience a *functional limitation* (FL). For example, physical performance may be limited in activities such as walking, climbing, reaching, and hearing; furthermore, the worker's emotional and mental performance may be adversely affected or limited.

Functional limitations, in turn, are likely to result in a disability, of which there are two types: *work disability* (WD) and *nonwork disability* (ND). Work disability can be thought of as having two phases: (1) *loss of earning capacity* (LEC), which results in (2) *actual wage loss* (AWL). In a strict sense, these two aspects of work disability must accompany one another. An actual loss of earnings occurs only if there is loss of earning capacity. Nevertheless, the distinction between the two phases is important because some types of workers' compensation benefits are based solely on a determination of a presumed loss of earning capacity, while other types of benefits require demonstration of actual wage loss.

Nonwork disability includes the loss of the capacity to engage in other aspects of everyday life, such as recreation and the performance of household tasks, and also can be thought of as having two phases: (1) *loss of capacity for nonwork activities* (LCNA), which results in (2) *actual noneconomic loss* (NEL). Again, in a strict sense, these two aspects of nonwork disability must accompany one another, but at least in principle they can be measured separately.

Determining What Should Be Compensated for Workers with Permanent Disabilities

The permanent consequences of injuries and diseases discussed in the previous section serve as a basis for the design of a PPD benefits system. One of the policy issues that must be resolved, implicitly or explicitly, in any jurisdiction designing a PPD system pertains to the purpose of the PPD benefits. Other policy issues include the operational approaches used to provide the PPD benefits and the disability rating system for PPD benefits.

The workers' compensation program's obligation to provide medical care and rehabilitation services is generally accepted (although in some jurisdictions,[1] including California, there is disagreement about the extent of vocational rehabilitation services to which a worker is entitled). Conversely, in most jurisdictions, there is general agreement that a worker is not entitled to benefits because of pain and suffering. The rationale often given for not compensating pain and suffering is that the original

---

[1] In this report, the terms "states," "provinces," and "jurisdictions" are used interchangeably.

design of workers' compensation involved a trade-off in which the employee was able to obtain benefits without demonstrating employer fault, and the employer's liability was limited to certain consequences of the injury, which did not encompass pain and suffering.

Most of the recent controversy over which of the permanent consequences of a work-related injury deserve compensation concerns the four permanent consequences shown in Figure 2.2. Because the four consequences are sequential and interdependent, a particular consequence may be endorsed as a basis for compensation because it serves as a convenient proxy for the other three. Thus, one may argue that impairment should be compensated when the real concern is for the work disability caused by the impairment. This indirect route to compensating work disability may be chosen because impairment may be easier to measure than work disability. Unfortunately, those who favor payment when a worker suffers an impairment do not always make clear whether the payment is meant to compensate for the existence of the impairment by itself or is meant to compensate for the work disability (or some other consequence) that is expected to result from the impairment.

To the extent that the rationale for benefits is discernable, however, two schools of thought can be identified. One school of thought views lost wages due to the injury (work disability) as the sole justification for workers' compensation benefits. Supporters of this position recognize that some jurisdictions pay benefits on the basis of an evaluation of the extent of impairment or an evaluation of some other permanent consequence shown in Figure 2.2 prior to actual wage loss, but also argue that when such evaluations are made, wage loss is conclusively presumed. The jurisdiction, in short, compensates on the basis of one of these intermediate consequences because the consequence of a work-related injury serves as a proxy for wage loss.

An alternative view of the rationale for benefits for workers with permanent consequences of work-related injuries accepts work disability as the primary basis for benefits, but argues that there is a secondary role for benefits paid for nonwork disability. Arguments for these "impairment benefits" state that the purpose of benefits is not only to compensate impairment per se but also to use permanent impairment as a convenient proxy for the functional limitations and nonwork disability that result from the impairment. A variant on this alternative view is that nonwork disability merits compensation, and that the degree of permanent impairment and/or functional limitations serves as a proxy for the extent of nonwork disability. The dominant view among jurisdictions probably is that the only permanent consequences that warrant benefits in a workers' compensation program are medical care, rehabilitation, and work disability. There are, however, several jurisdictions that have explicitly adopted benefits for nonwork disability, including Florida (which paid what were termed "permanent impairment" benefits from 1979 to 1993) and most Canadian provinces, such as Ontario (which pays noneconomic loss benefits).

The pre–SB 899 California rationale for permanent disability benefits was stated in Labor Code Section 4660:

> . . . account shall be taken of the nature of the physical injury or disfigurement, the occupation of the injured employee, and his age at the time of such injury, consideration being given to the diminished ability of such injured employee to compete in an open labor market.

This statutory language clearly appears to indicate that the purpose of the PPD benefits in California is to compensate for work disability and not for nonwork disability. We therefore assume for the remainder of this report that the sole purpose of the PPD benefits in California is to compensate work disability, and we base our evaluation of the state's PPD benefits on this assumption. In the next section, we examine the criteria for the evaluation of the California PPD benefits based on this assumption that the sole purpose of the benefits is to compensate injured workers for the extent of their work disability.

As noted in Chapter One, amended Section 4660 of SB 899 replaced the language "the diminished ability of such injured employee to compete in an open labor market" with "the employee's diminished future earning capacity." This change retains, and may indeed strengthen, the emphasis on work disability over nonwork disability in California's permanent disability system.

Criteria for Evaluating PPD Benefits

The most prominent comprehensive evaluation of workers' compensation systems in the United States is *The Report of the National Commission on State Workmen's Compensation Laws* (the *National Commission Report*), which was published in 1972. The *National Commission Report* (National Commission on State Workmen's Compensation Laws, 1972) primarily relies on the following two criteria to evaluate workers' compensation programs:

1. *Adequate*, which the *National Commission Report* (p. 15) defines as "sufficient to meet the needs or objectives of the program; thus [one examines] whether the resources being devoted to workmen's compensation income benefits are sufficient."

2. *Equitable*, which the *National Commission Report* (p. 15) defines as "fair or just; thus [one examines] whether workers with similar disabilities resulting from work-related injuries or diseases are treated similarly by different States."

Benefit Adequacy

The meaning of the *adequacy criterion* can be explained by referring to the *National Commission Report*. The National Commission did not make specific recommendations for PPD benefits that would permit a translation of providing "substantial protection against interruption of income" into a numerical or quantitative standard. However, for TTD and permanent total disability, the National Commission recommended, subject to the state's maximum weekly benefits, that the disability benefits be at least two-thirds of the worker's pre-injury gross weekly wage.

The National Commission also recommended that beneficiaries in permanent total disability cases have their benefits increased through time in the same proportion as increases in the state's average weekly wage. If a similar degree of protection were provided for permanent partial disability as for permanent total disability, then after the date of MMI, the PPD benefits should replace two-thirds of the difference between the worker's *potential earnings* (the earnings that a worker would have earned had he or she not been injured) and the worker's actual earnings. Alternatively stated, benefits are adequate if the *replacement rate*—the PPD benefits divided by the earnings losses experienced by an injured worker—is at least 66-2/3 percent. A National Academy of Social Insurance report on the adequacy of permanent partial disability benefits (Hunt, 2004) cites the replacement rate of 66-2/3 percent (or two-thirds) of lost wages (measured before payroll deductions for taxes or other items) as the measure of adequacy.

Past RAND studies, most notably Peterson et al. (1997) and Reville et al. (2001c), have directed much attention to whether or not PPD benefits in California are adequate. The general conclusion of these studies is that replacement rates may be adequate when viewed over a relatively short period of time, say two or three years, but over a longer period of time, such as five or ten years, replacement rates fall short of the two-thirds adequacy level. Recent reform efforts in California (specifically, Assembly Bill (AB) 749, which was signed into law in February 2002) have led to increases in PPD benefits in an effort to improve the adequacy of those benefits, although when inflation is taken into account, the recent increases largely restored benefits to levels that were paid in the early 1990s (see Boden, Reville, and Biddle, 2005). SB 899 also decreased benefits for low-rated claims (which are more common than higher-rated claims), and increased benefits for higher-rated claims, which when combined with the other changes discussed here will produce an average effect that is uncertain.

Benefit Equity

We begin our discussion of the *equitable criterion* by distinguishing between *horizontal equity* and *vertical equity*. Horizontal equity requires that workers who are equivalent should be treated equally. In other words, if the purpose of PPD benefits is to compensate for loss of earnings, then for benefits to exhibit horizontal equity workers with equal earnings losses should receive equal benefits. If workers A and B both have $1,000 of earnings losses, and worker A receives $700 in benefits (and, therefore, has a 70 percent replacement rate) and worker B receives $300 in benefits (a 30 percent replacement rate), then the assignment of PPD benefits will have failed the horizontal equity test.

Vertical equity, in a narrow sense, requires that workers with differing losses of income should receive benefits proportional to their losses. If worker C has $5,000 of earnings losses and $3,000 of benefits, while worker D has $10,000 of earnings losses, then the narrow test of vertical equity requires that worker D receive $6,000 of benefits (so that the replacement rate for both workers is 60 percent). A more general test for vertical equity only requires that there be a positive correlation between losses and benefits. Under this definition, benefits would pass the test for vertical equity as long as worker D had PPD benefits greater than $3,000. In reality, the optimal level of vertical equity is probably somewhere between the two extremes. Perhaps it is unreasonable to expect benefits to increase on a one-to-one basis with earnings losses, but there should be a reasonably close relationship between the two.

The ability of a state's workers' compensation program to provide benefits that meet the horizontal and vertical tests for equity depend in large part on the rating system for PPD benefits used by the state. The purpose of the rating system is to incorporate all the relevant information about a case and convert it into benefits. Thus, PPD benefits will be assigned in an equitable fashion only if the disabilities are rated in an equitable fashion. A large part of this study focuses on analyzing the effect to which permanent disabilities in California are rated in an equitable fashion.

Another aspect of the equity criterion, in addition to horizontal and vertical equity, is the *consistency* with which benefits are assigned. Simply put, consistency requires that workers with similar disabilities and similar outcomes be repeatedly assigned the same benefits. Consider a hypothetical worker E who has earnings losses equal to $6,000 and a system that targets the two-thirds replacement rate. Suppose that ten different physicians each evaluate worker E separately, and each time a disability rating is assigned. If the system is perfectly consistent, then worker E should be assigned benefits of $4,000 each time. In Chapter Seven of this report we examine the consistency, or rather the inconsistency, with which disability ratings are assigned in the California system.

Additional Criteria for Evaluation

In this section, we briefly discuss three additional criteria that will bear on our discussion of the implications of SB 899 and possible additional reforms. However, we do not have sufficient data to address these issues as comprehensively as other issues covered in this report. For further information on these criteria, see Burton (1997).

Delivery System Efficiency

This criterion concerns the proper relationship between two elements of the workers' compensation system: the administrative costs of providing the benefits of the workers' compensation program and the quality of those benefits, as measured by other criteria such as adequacy and equity.[2] *Delivery system efficiency* implies that benefits of a given quality (in terms of adequacy and equity) are provided at minimum cost.

In this report, the question of delivery system efficiency arises in the discussion of the possibility that the California rating system leads to increased litigation (see Chapter Seven). Litigation imposes costs on participants, including attorney's fees, medical-legal expenses, and system administrative costs (e.g., court costs). However, as a general rule, it likely that litigation improves benefits for an individual injured worker and thus could have a positive effect on the adequacy and equity of the system (although equity might not be improved if there is an uneven distribution of the availability of quality legal representation). Nevertheless, the permanent disability rating is intended as an administrative replacement to the determination of benefits through adversarial advocacy. Given the rating, the adequacy is then set by statute. Therefore, while litigation over many issues in workers' compensation can improve outcomes for injured workers, and while litigation over a disability rating may improve outcomes for a particular injured worker, we argue that litigation over the disability rating is inefficient and contrary to the intended purpose of an administrative system based upon permanent disability ratings.

Prevention, Compensation, and Rehabilitation (PCR) System Efficiency

This criterion concerns avoiding unintended side effects from PPD benefits on all the objectives of the PCR system for workers, such as the prevention of work-related and nonwork-related injuries and diseases, the provision of appropriate medical care and cash benefits for disabled workers, and the rehabilitation and reemployment of those workers.

In this report, the issue of PCR system efficiency arises in the context of whether the approach to permanent disability benefits encourages or discourages return to employment by the injured worker (see Chapter Six).

Affordability

This criterion concerns designing a system of PPD benefits that employers, workers, and the public can afford without serious adverse consequences, such as a significant loss of jobs.

---

[2] Berkowitz and Burton (1987, pp. 26–27) included *efficiency* as a third criterion for evaluating permanent disability benefits. Efficiency was termed *delivery system efficiency* in Burton (1997, p. 14), which also included the two other additional criteria discussed in this section—*prevention, compensation, and rehabilitation (PCR) system efficiency* and *affordability*—in evaluating benefits.

There is a danger in adding to the number of criteria used to evaluate PPD benefits—that an already complex evaluation process will become even more complex. This is particularly true because the criteria often come into conflict in evaluating PPD benefit systems, and the more criteria in use, the greater the number of conflicts and trade-offs that must be considered.

We are, however, persuaded that all five criteria are important considerations when designing policy to compensate for PPD. "Efficiency" is a term that has been used by some economists to include what we term "administrative efficiency" and "prevention, compensation, and rehabilitation system efficiency," and the explicit difference in these terms should help in distinguishing between the two meanings of efficiency. "Affordability" has seldom been explicitly mentioned as a criteria, but has always been an implicit criteria lurking in the background. Indeed, in recent years, affordability may have de facto become the dominant criterion in the reform of PPD benefits in a number of states, including California, and explicit recognition of affordability as a criterion may improve the policy debates concerning efforts to reform the PPD benefits system.

Summary: Using the Criteria to Evaluate the California System

The goal of this chapter was to outline a framework for thinking about past and current debates on PPD. We argue that California, like most states, explicitly chooses to compensate permanently disabled workers based on their diminished earnings capacity. Our discussion here has provided numerous criteria that must be considered when designing a system to provide this compensation. In the subsequent chapters of this report, we discuss various methods for implementing a compensation system for PPD, and we then proceed to evaluate the California system using the criteria discussed here.

Of the many criteria discussed here, the one that we focus on in our empirical evaluation is equity, primarily because that is the only one that we can directly address with our data. Past RAND studies have addressed the issue of adequacy, but, unfortunately, the issues of efficiency and affordability are and will remain open questions until further data collection becomes possible. Simply by means of comparison with other states, it is easy to look at the California system and assert that it is neither efficient nor affordable. However, it is considerably more challenging to determine which individual parts of the system need to be changed, and how to change them. One might argue that a part of the system, such as the rating schedule, is inefficient or increases costs, but ultimately these arguments are based on logic (or anecdote) and not on empirical evidence.

It is also important to keep in mind that in some cases the various evaluation criteria may conflict with one another. As mentioned earlier, increases in benefits may make the system better off in terms of adequacy but worse off in terms of affordability. This fact will be particularly relevant when considering the empirical results we present in Chapters Five, Six, and Seven. In some cases, we might find that disability ratings fail one of the equity criteria, such as horizontal equity, but this could be justified by other objectives (such as promoting efficiency). We do our best to point out such considerations where they are merited, but the reader should keep in mind that with such a complex issue no single evaluation criterion is comprehensive enough to definitively determine whether or not the system performs well.

Finally, we conclude this chapter by noting that evaluating the equity of disability ratings is not necessarily the same as evaluating the equity of disability benefits. Ultimately, disability ratings are important only because of their use in distributing benefits to injured workers. An equitable and consistent ratings system is necessary but not sufficient to guarantee equitable and consistent benefits. For instance, a ratings system might be vertically equitable in the sense that workers with higher disability ratings suffer higher losses, but benefits will be equitable only if they are tied to ratings in an appropriate manner. We focus the majority of our attention in this report on evaluating the ratings system, but acknowledge that this system is just one part of a larger analysis of the appropriateness of the compensation for disabled workers.

CHAPTER THREE

Evaluating and Rating Permanent Disabilities in California

Any compensation scheme for PPD benefits must start with a system to rate the extent of permanent impairment suffered by the injured workers. Most states now use some edition of the *AMA Guides* (American Medical Association, 2000) to produce an impairment rating that is then used in conjunction with other information to determine the amount of PPD benefits. Prior to SB 899, California had a unique system for determining the extent of impairment. The California rating schedule is complex and the history of it is tangled; therefore, we only summarize aspects of the rating schedule in this chapter.[1] In the new post–SB 899 system, impairment will be measured using the criteria in the *AMA Guides*, but these ratings will be adjusted to reflect average earnings losses across various impairments. As of this writing, there are a number of uncertainties about how certain elements of SB 899 will be applied and implemented, preventing us from giving a detailed account of disability ratings under the new system. Our discussion in this chapter focuses on the California system before the new reforms, which is the relevant system for the data we used in our empirical analyses in this study. Portions of this discussion were reported previously in Berkowitz and Burton (1987).

In the remainder of this report, we refer to the permanent disability rating system that existed prior to SB 899 as the "rating system" or the "California system," because it was unique to California. In fact, the new permanent disability rating system also is unique to California. However, to avoid confusion, we refer to the new system as the "SB 899 system."

Overview and History of the California Rating System

The California approach to determining the extent of permanent partial disability has traditionally been unusual, if not unique, among American workers' compensa-

---

[1] More extensive discussions on this subject are in Welch (1973, chapter titled "Permanent Disability Evaluation"), Welch (1964), and the California Senate Interim Committee (1953, Part I). Eli P. Welch was chief of the Permanent Disability Rating Bureau.

tion programs. For one thing, the California workers' compensation statute does not include a traditional rating schedule with a list of body members (e.g., arm, leg, hand, foot) and a corresponding duration of benefits associated with total loss or loss of use of each of the body members.[2] Instead, the statute gives the administrative director of the Division of Workers' Compensation the authority to adopt a rating schedule for the determination of the severity of disability.

Moreover, the California system has been unusual in that its rating schedule traditionally considered factors other than the nature and severity of an injury in determining the degree of disability. These factors, the procedure for adopting the schedule, and the significance of the schedule are included in statutory language that had been largely unchanged since 1917, when the original 1914 statute was amended to require consideration of the worker's diminished ability to compete in an open labor market when determining the percentage of permanent disability.[3] That 1917 statutory language is as follows:

> Section 4660. (a) In determining the percentages of permanent disability, account shall be taken of the nature of the physical injury or disfigurement, the occupation of the injured employee, and his age at the time of such injury, consideration being given to the diminished ability of such injured employee to compete in an open labor market.
>
> (b) The administrative director may prepare, adopt, and from time to time amend a schedule for the determination of the percentage of permanent disabilities in accordance with this section. Such a schedule shall be available for public inspection, and without formal introduction in evidence shall be *prima facie* evidence of the percentage of permanent disability to be attributed to each injury covered by the schedule.

The 1914 California schedule used a hypothetical "standard man" as a reference point for the occupational and age adjustments made to the standard rating of an injury. The standard occupation was ditch digger. For the standard age, the 1910 census in California was used. After certain actuarial adjustments were made, the average worker was found to be 39 years old. Thus, the worker used as the standard in the 1914 schedule was a 39-year-old ditch digger (laborer).

---

[2] While the California workers' compensation statute does not include a schedule with the duration of PPD benefits associated with the loss of or loss of use of particular body parts, Section 4662 of the California Labor Code conclusively presumes that certain types of impairments (such as loss of both hands or incurable insanity) constitute permanent total disability. Most states have similar provisions that represent a statutory schedule of particularly serous injuries that are presumed to result in permanent total disability.

[3] The only other change in the language of Section 4660 (a) and (b) of the Labor Code prior to SB 899 was made in 1966, when authority to prepare, adopt, and amend the schedule was transferred from the Industrial Accident Commission (the predecessor of the Workers' Compensation Appeals Board) to the administrative director of the Division of Industrial Accidents.

The 1914 schedule contained 52 occupational classifications. The standard rating was increased or decreased depending on whether the physical demands for each occupation were considered relatively greater or less than those for the ditch digger for the particular part of the body involved. Similarly, if the worker were over 39, the disability rating was increased, and if the worker was under 39, the rating was decreased. Thus, the 1914 schedule determined for each case a permanent disability rating based on the nature of the worker's injury, the particular occupation, and the worker's age at the time of injury.

Minor amendments were made in the 1914 schedule before World War II.[4] After World War II, because of concerns that the schedule might have become outdated, an extensive review of the California permanent disability rating system and of alternative rating procedures was conducted, and a report was submitted to the Industrial Accident Commission (the predecessor of the Workers' Compensation Appeals Board) in 1947. The 1950 revision that resulted did not disturb the basic concepts found in the 1914 schedule. The hypothetical standard worker, on whom the occupational adjustments are based, had been a laborer in the original schedule, but this specific occupation was abandoned in favor of a generalized occupation, with average physical demands on all parts of the body. The occupational section contained more than 1,800 occupations, which were assigned to 61 occupational groups (Swezey, 2003, Section 5.36). The age of 39 was retained as the standard, and ratings continued to be adjusted upward for older workers and downward for younger workers. Additionally, there were some revisions in the standard ratings for injuries "in the light of analysis and Mr. Haggard's [superintendent of the Permanent Disability Rating Bureau] experience" (Welch, 1964, p. 18).

The 1950 schedule was used with some minor amendments until the 1990s. When Berkowitz and Burton (1987) conducted their fieldwork in the 1980s, the California workers' compensation program was relying on the 1978 edition of the schedule, which was 82 pages long. It was supplemented by a rule of the administrative director (Section 9725) that the objective factors of disability (discussed later in this chapter) be rated by methods described in a standard text. The schedule also incorporated "work capacity guidelines" for the evaluation of troublesome injuries (such as back, heart, and pulmonary injuries). Use of these various measures allowed every injury and disease to be rated.

Section 4660 of the Labor Code was amended in 1993 to add subsection (d), which required the administrative director to review and revise the schedule in order to update the standard disability ratings and occupations to reflect the current labor market. The result was a new *Schedule for Rating Permanent Disabilities* (hereafter *1997 Rating Schedule*) (Division of Workers' Compensation, 1997) that was effective

---

[4] There were 14 amendments by 1939, according to Welch (1964, p. 16).

for injuries occurring on and after April 1, 1997. This new rating schedule was 90 pages long. The number of occupational groups was reduced from 61 to 44, and each group was given a three-digit number. The first digit represents the arduousness of the occupation based on the physical demands on the particular body part based on the description of the job in the *Dictionary of Occupational Titles*. The age table in the 1955 schedule relied on two-year intervals, which were changed to five-year intervals in the *1997 Rating Schedule*. However, the age 39 was retained as the standard age (Swezey, 2003, Section 5.38).

Despite these changes, the approach of the *1997 Rating Schedule* remained essentially identical to the approach of the 1955 schedule, which, in turn, was an obvious descendant of the 1914 schedule. This is important for our purposes, because the data we use in our analysis in the following chapters include only cases that were rated under the pre-1997 schedule. Given that most of the approach is the same, however, the results should be applicable, at least in a broad sense, to all injuries rated prior to the new reforms. Unfortunately, because our data include only the pre-1997 occupation categories, we are unable to provide a thorough evaluation of the effectiveness of the current occupation adjustments. We do provide a limited analysis in Appendix C.

SB 899 amended Section 4660 once again, as noted above. The impairment descriptions were changed (and, thus, so too was the use of work-capacity guidelines); the descriptions were among other unique aspects of California's system. However, the occupational and age adjustments of the *1997 Rating Schedule* were unchanged by the legislation.

Application of the California Schedule

Under the *1997 Rating Schedule*, each injury is given a standard rating based on observable medical factors. For example, the loss of one leg at or above the ankle but below the knee receives a standard disability rating of 50 percent (assuming satisfactory use of a prosthesis).[5] The standard rating, modified by the occupational and age adjustments, is used to determine the amount of permanent disability benefits that the injured worker receives.

Often, the determination of a standard rating under the California system has been more difficult than the example of the leg amputation suggests. This is due in part to the fact that the system has included three sets of criteria for rating permanent disabilities: objective factors, subjective factors, and work-capacity guidelines (Swezey, 2003, Sections 5.41–5.43). We describe the application of these sets of factors in turn.

---

[5] This example is from Swezey (2003, Section 5.48).

Objective Factors

The measurement of objective factors in the California rating system is based upon Thurber (1960). The Thurber reference volume resulted from an effort in 1940 to establish some uniformity in the measurement of impairments. It had become obvious by then that doctors were arriving at widely varying assessments of the extent of impairment for similar or identical injuries, resulting in widely varying standard disability ratings for identical or similar injuries. A committee chaired by Dr. Packard Thurber, with representatives from the California Medical Association, the Industrial Accident Commission, and other agencies, prepared the new guidelines for evaluation. The committee based its work on several principles: the guidelines should be brief and not unduly complicated; the evaluation procedures already used by the Industrial Accident Commission should be followed as much as possible; and, finally, the relevant concept for determining restricted motion was the worker's remaining active (or functional) motion, not his or her passive motion.[6]

The descriptions of the methods used in the California workers' compensation program to assess impairments and rate their severity appear to be rather cursory. Section 2 of the *1997 Rating Schedule* contains 19 pages that provide instructions about how to determine the disability ratings for specific medical conditions. Section 7 of the *1997 Rating Schedule* contains an additional nine pages devoted to rating specific conditions, plus instructions about how to combine multiple disabilities. Additional assistance in rating disabilities is provided in the *Physician's Guide to Medical Practice in the California Workers' Compensation System, Third Edition* (Industrial Medical Council, 2001), which devotes seven pages (pp. 41–47) to guidelines for conducting a disability evaluation. On pages 42–43 of the *Physician's Guide*, doctors are told, "The Industrial Medical Council's evaluation protocols (see Appendix C for more information) and Packard Thurber's Evaluation of Industrial Disability detail how the findings, such as range of motion, should be presented." The Industrial Medical Council's evaluation protocols (in its *Evaluation Guidelines*) are available for six types of injuries: cardio, neuromusculoskeletal, foot and ankle, psychiatric, immunologic, and pulmonary (Industrial Medical Council, 2003).

The comprehensiveness of the rating guidelines in the California workers' compensation program varies among the types of injuries, but in general appears to be limited when compared with the *AMA Guides*. For example, consider the guidelines for upper extremities. Eight pages (pages 2-7 through 2-11 and appendix pages 7-4 through 7-6) in the *1997 Rating Schedule* explain how to rate shoulders and arms, amputations, limited motion of fingers, and hand-grip strength. The *Physician's*

---

[6] The Thurber volume differs from the *AMA Guides* in several ways. Thurber is confined to assessment of injuries to the musculoskeletal system, whereas the *AMA Guides* deal with all body systems, including the cardiovascular and digestive systems. For the musculoskeletal system, the Thurber approach is roughly the same as the *AMA Guides* approach; they both concentrate on the objective manifestations of impairment, such as restricted motion or ankylosis.

Guide and the *Evaluation Guides* published by the Industrial Medical Council contain no further instructions for rating upper extremities.[7] In contrast, the chapter dealing with upper extremities in the fifth edition of the *AMA Guides* (Chapter 16) is 89 pages long.

Subjective Factors

The California permanent disability rating schedules traditionally have considered subjective manifestations of impairment in evaluating injuries. These "subjective factors" (Swezey, 2003, Section 5.42), as they are known in California, were among the sources of controversy in the recent SB 899 reforms. The guidelines for considering the subjective manifestations are explained in Section 9727 of the Rules issued by the administrative director of the Division of Industrial Accidents:

> Section 9727. *Subjective Disability.* Subjective Disability should be identified by:
> • A description of the activity that produces disability.
> • The duration of the disability.
> • The activities that are precluded and those that can be performed with the disability.
> • The means necessary for relief.
>
> The terms shown below are presumed to mean the following:[8]
> • A *severe pain* would preclude the activity precipitating the pain.
> • A *moderate pain* could be tolerated, but would cause a marked handicap in the performance of the activity precipitating the pain.
> • A *slight pain* could be tolerated, but would cause some handicap in the performance of the activity precipitating the pain.
> • A *minimal (mild) pain* would constitute an annoyance, but because it causes no handicap in the performance of the particular activity, it would be considered a non-ratable permanent disability.

The *1997 Rating Schedule* (Division of Workers' Compensation, 1997, pp. 1–7) indicates that the frequency of pain is also relevant in evaluating injuries and provides the following definitions: "*constant*—90–100 percent [of the time]; *frequent*—75 percent [of the time]; *intermittent*—50 percent [of the time]; and *occasional*—25 percent [of the time]."

The *1997 Rating Schedule* lists a number of injuries evaluated on the basis of subjective factors. The range of standard disability ratings for injuries evaluated on this basis can be considerable: several injuries, such as paralysis of one side of the

---

[7] *Guidelines for Evaluation of Neuromusculoskeletal Evaluation Disability* published by the Industrial Medical Council (2003) addresses low-back and neck injuries.

[8] In this chapter, we discuss how pain is assessed in the California system to determine disability ratings. In the next chapter, we discuss how chronic pain is assessed in the *AMA Guides* and IMC Guidelines, which differ from the California guidelines.

body, receive 20 percent ratings for "slight" disability and 100 percent for "severe" disability. Despite the language of Section 9727, the schedule does not confine consideration of the subjective factors to pain,[9] nor are the only ratable categories "slight," "moderate," and "severe." Headaches receive a standard rating of 5 percent if the pain is slight; a 15 percent rating if it is moderate; 60 percent if it is severe; and 100 percent if it is pronounced (Division of Workers' Compensation, 1997, p. 2-2). Epilepsy also contains the category "slight to moderate," which receives a standard rating of 50 percent. "Moderate" epilepsy receives a standard rating of 75 percent, and because a rating may be increased or decreased from the scheduled ratings when the degree of impairment warrants it, epilepsy more serious than "slight to moderate" but less serious than "moderate" might be rated as a 60 percent or 65 percent disability.

Part of the impetus for the use of work-capacity guidelines in place of the subjective disability approach was a 1953 report of the California Senate Interim Committee. A section in the report entitled "Incredible Inconsistencies in Rating Specialists' Computations" states the following:

> The claim by the rating specialists of the commission that ratings are consistent, one with another, is pure fiction. Called upon separately by us to rate a set of hypothetical cases, two specialists arrived at amazingly different rates. The test cases included twelve (12) disabilities of varying degrees of severity, each case to be rated for four (4) different occupations and all cases at age 39 years. For not one of these forty-eight (48) cases did the specialists arrive at the same rating . . . . For the forty-eight (48) cases, the average difference between ratings is 12.05 percent; the average difference in payment periods, 48 weeks; and in terms of cash benefits, the average difference between cases (at $30 per week) is $1,440 (California Senate Interim Committee, 1953, pp. 60–62).

The California Senate Interim Committee selected 24 actual ratings from case files. These cases were resubmitted to the same ratings specialist who made the original computations. Three of the cases showed the same percentage as indicated in the original rating, but six re-ratings were higher than the original ratings and 11 were lower. The other four cases involved some change between the original rating and the re-rating.

Although the California Senate Interim Committee did not confine its criticism to ratings involving subjective disability, the committee obviously was concerned about the subjective rating system,[10] and the criticism was probably an important fac-

---

[9] The *1997 Rating Schedule* (Division of Workers' Compensation, 1997, pp. 1–7) states, "Subjective residuals of an injury may include pain, numbness, weakness, tenderness, paresthesia, and sensitivity."

[10] As stated in a committee report, ". . . 'slight,' 'moderate,' and 'severe' have different meanings to different persons involved in the judicial process of the commission. What may be 'slight,' 'moderate,' or 'severe' as the case may be, to litigants and referees alike, may prove to be something different to the rating specialist although pre-

tor in the development of the work-capacity guidelines.

The subjective factors can be considered examples of subjective manifestations of impairment. They expand the California criteria for evaluating permanent disability beyond the factors considered by the *AMA Guides* or by Thurber (1960). There is, however, no published guide to aid in the evaluation of subjective factors other than the descriptions "severe," "moderate," "slight," and "minimal" contained in Section 9727 of the administrative director's Rules.

Work-Capacity Guidelines

According to Swezey (2003, Section 5.43), work-capacity guidelines were developed in the 1950s by the state Ratings Bureau to overcome a lack of uniformity and consistency in ratings. Welch (1973, Section 15.17) provides an example of the ratings problems the guidelines were designed to address:

> Initially, the schedule provided only three ratings for the spine: slight (30%), moderate (50%), and severe (100%). It did not define these levels, and obviously all spinal disabilities could not be rated on only these three points. The guidelines were evolved to permit more precise ratings on spinal disabilities, and the definitions of work capacity were developed in relation to spinal disabilities only.

Since the 1950s, the work-capacity guidelines have been extended to other types of injuries, but their origin as a method to rate disabilities of the spine is evident. The work-capacity guidelines developed in the 1950s had eight levels, or "plateaus," of disability. Four of the plateaus were described as follows by Berkowitz and Burton (1987, p.178):

(a) *"Disability precluding very heavy lifting*—contemplates the individual has lost approximately one-quarter of his pre-injury capacity for lifting." This disability receives a standard rating of 10 percent. A note to this guideline says, "A statement 'inability to lift 50 pounds' is not meaningful. The total lifting effort, including weight, distance, endurance, frequency, body position, and similar factors should be considered with reference to the particular individual."
(e) *"Disability precluding heavy work*—contemplates the individual has lost approximately half of his pre-injury capacity for performing such activities as bending, stooping, lifting, pushing, pulling, and climbing, or other activities involving comparable physical effort." This disability receives a standard rating of 30 percent.
(g) *"Disability resulting in limitation to semi-sedentary work*—contemplates the individual can do work approximately one half the time in a sitting position,

sumably the latter also functions under the same legislative formula and rules of evidence" (California Senate Interim Committee, 1953, p. 42).

and approximately one half the time in a standing or walking position, with a minimum of demands for physical effort whether standing, walking, or sitting." This disability receives a standard rating of 60 percent.

(h) "*Disability resulting in limitation to sedentary work*—contemplates that the individual can do work predominantly in a sitting position at a bench, desk, or table with a minimum of demands for physical effort and with some degree of walking and standing being permitted." This disability receives a standard rating of 70 percent.

The Disability Evaluation Bureau used the predecessors to these guidelines informally since the 1950s, first to rate spinal injuries and later to rate a few additional categories of injuries. The guidelines were formally incorporated into the *Schedule for Rating Permanent Disabilities* for injuries occurring on and after January 1, 1970, for chronic infections of pulmonary tissues, heart disability, spinal disabilities, and abdominal weakness. Following an appellate court decision, the two plateaus representing the most severe disabilities (g and h above) were added to the schedule as a basis for evaluating injuries to the lower extremities that occurred on or after January 1, 1973.

The *1997 Rating Schedule* expanded the scope of the work-capacity guidelines (Swezey, 2003, Section 5.43). There are now 12 work-capacity guidelines for lower extremity injuries (Division of Workers' Compensation, 1997, p. 2-19), ten work-capacity guidelines for the spine and torso, and three work-capacity guidelines based on subjective factors for the spine and torso (Division of Workers' Compensation, 1997, pp. 2-14–2-15).

Several components of the work-capacity guidelines do not displace, but only supplement or complement, the subjective rating factors in the *1997 Rating Schedule*. First, the work-capacity guidelines for the spine and torso provide alternative methods to obtain a standard rating of 10 percent—either a work-capacity rating of "disability precluding very heavy lifting" or a subjective factor rating of "constant slight pain." Moreover, disability to the neck, back of pelvis has a standard rating of 100 percent with a subjective factor rating of "severe," and this 100 percent rating can be given even though the maximum plateau in the work-capacity guidelines is a 70 percent standard rating.

Second, aside from the use of the subjective factors as an alternative to the work-capacity guidelines, the guidelines themselves can be approached in two ways—in terms of the work restrictions specified by the plateau designations (e.g., "disability precluding heavy work") or in terms of the activities that the worker can still do after an injury or can no longer do because of an injury ("contemplates the individual has lost approximately half of his pre-injury capacity for performing such activities as bending, stooping, lifting . . .").

However, none of this describes what is actually being evaluated by the work-capacity guidelines. We can consider the objective factors to be objective manifestations of impairment. The work-capacity guidelines are not so easy to classify. The guidelines' descriptions of certain precluded activities correspond to functional limitations—that is, limitations in general (or nonwork-specific) activities, such as walking, climbing, and bending. However, most of the plateau designations (for example, "disability resulting in limitation to semi-sedentary work") and some of the guidelines' descriptions (for example, the descriptions of plateaus g and h above) correspond to work disability. Thus, the quest for more consistency in evaluating injuries as a result of the criticism of the use of subjective factors led to more categories (12 plateaus in place of the three levels of subjective disability included in Section 9727 of the Rules) and the use of criteria that consider the consequences of injury farther downstream in the injury, impairment, functional limitations, disability sequence shown in Figure 2.2 in Chapter Two.

Final Points

Some additional elaboration on the rating of permanent disabilities is warranted. First, "objective factors," "subjective factors," and "work-capacity guidelines" are not mutually exclusive categories. Rather, it is quite common for an injury to have rating factors from more than one category, such as an injury to the wrist that causes immobility plus pain.[11]

Second, the discussion in this chapter on the use of the rating schedule indicated that some opportunities exist for the exercise of discretion in the rating of injuries. To a much more limited extent, a workers' compensation judge (in some cases with the assistance of a disability evaluation specialist) has some discretion in the choice of the occupation to be used in adjusting the standard rating. This situation is more likely to arise if the worker is in an occupation that does not appear on the list of occupations in the *1997 Rating Schedule.* The judge or the specialist can then turn to a brief set of rules in the *1997 Rating Schedule* (on page I-14), which is used to assign nonscheduled occupations to an appropriate occupational group based on job functions and physical demands.

Conclusion

The need for more objective and consistent ratings has been a recurring theme in California workers' compensation policy. The ratings schedule has gone through multiple revisions that were intended to make the ratings more objective and consistent. In Chapter Seven, we show that, despite these revisions, consistency remained a

---

[11] This example is from Swezey (2003, Section 5.49).

significant problem for the *1997 Rating Guide*. To make the ratings more objective, SB 899 replaced the objective, subjective, and work-capacity guidelines with the descriptions of impairment that are used in the *AMA Guides*. The *AMA Guides* are concerned primarily with objective manifestations of impairment, but the California schedule considers subjective manifestations of impairment ("subjective factors") and functional limitations and work disabilities ("work-capacity guidelines"). In this sense, the California criteria for rating permanent disabilities are much more extensive than those of the *AMA Guides*. However, the *AMA Guides* are at least as broad, if not broader, than the California criteria in terms of the number of body systems covered. The objective factors in the California schedule are largely confined to the musculoskeletal system; factors related to body systems other than the musculoskeletal system is often cursory or incomplete. The *AMA Guides*, on the other hand, devote chapters to the digestive, reproductive, and urinary systems, which are not even covered by the California schedule. In practice, injuries or diseases that affect these body systems may be compensable in California as nonscheduled disabilities.[12] But the *1997 Rating Schedule* by itself is a limited guide to the evaluation of permanent impairment as compared with the *AMA Guides*.[13]

This chapter summarized a number of key points about the California permanent disability rating system, including a comparison of several aspects of the state's rating system and the *AMA Guides*. In the next chapter, we delve into an important consideration for both the *AMA Guides* and the California rating system: how to evaluate and assess chronic pain.

---

[12] This is in part because the California rating schedule is designed to measure an injured workers' diminished capacity to compete in the labor market. Some injuries, such as an impaired reproductive system, may not affect earnings capacity and, therefore, are not included in the schedule but may still be compensable.

[13] There are also serious limitations to the *AMA Guides*, as discussed in Spieler et al. (2000).

CHAPTER FOUR
Evaluation of Chronic Pain for Workers' Compensation

Perhaps the most controversial aspect of California's permanent disability rating system relates to disability ratings for chronic pain. The California disability rating system has attempted to compensate chronic pain, through both the use of subjective criteria and work capacity guidelines. In this chapter, we discuss the assessment of chronic pain in the California system and compare it with the *AMA Guides* (American Medical Association, 2000), which became the new standard for rating disabilities under SB 899.

Chronic pain refers to long-lasting painful sensations that may, or may not, accompany a well-defined physical lesion or pathology. Unlike *acute pain,* which can often be attributed to an immediate physical injury, chronic pain is more ambiguous in its origins, mechanisms, and manifestations. The physiological basis and legitimacy of chronic pain remain subjects of controversy among physicians. Conventional notions that have distinguished between psychogenic[1] and organic origins for pain are being challenged by newer theories that recognize the limits of mind-body dualism in explaining pain sensations. Scientific progress in understanding chronic pain is relevant to the California workers' compensation system in two ways. First, fundamental legal distinctions about the compensability of injuries—physical versus psychiatric—may break down, given that some chronic pain cases may defy classification into one of those two categories. Second, medical-legal standards for the evaluation of pain-related disability may be fundamentally ambiguous and inconsistent to such a degree as to limit the validity and reliability of ratings of impairment (American Medical Association, 2000, pp. 568–569). Even the threshold determination of whether a legitimate medical disability exists at all may sometimes call for subjective judgment on the part of an evaluating physician.

The purpose of this chapter is briefly to describe current medical theories for chronic pain and to examine the evaluation guidelines for chronic pain provided by the AMA and the California Industrial Medical Council (IMC) for use in the Cali-

---

[1] The term *psychogenic* is used here to refer to a pain sensation that is caused by psychological factors, in the absence of a biological cause. See the *AMA Guides* (American Medical Association, 2000, pp. 568–569).

fornia disability rating system (prior to SB 899). This chapter concludes with a discussion of the implications of this comparison, in light of the importance of chronic pain as a major category of disability among workers' compensation claimants.[2]

Theories of Pain

The International Association for the Study of Pain defines *pain* as "an unpleasant sensory or emotional experience associated with actual or potential tissue damage, or described in terms of such damage" (Merskey, 1986). Pain is essentially experiential in its character and is therefore distinct from any physical injury that may give rise to it. Setting aside colloquial use of the word to refer to unpleasant emotional experience (e.g., bereavement), "pain" is typically associated with a perception of bodily damage, dysfunction, or distress. The observed association between pain and physical damage originally gave rise to a theory of simple causation, with pain viewed as a physical concomitant to organic injury or pathology.[3] In the 1950s, pain was understood primarily as a *proportional* response to injury or pathology, and pain observed in the absence of identified physical harm was frequently viewed as a psychiatric problem (Melzack, 1999b). Terms such as "conversion disorder," "hysteria," and "psychogenic pain" were all used to refer to "psychiatric" pains, which were typically construed as subjective in nature and psychological in origin. Some of these terms continue to be used to describe or to refer to nonorganic pains.[4]

Researchers began to become dissatisfied with traditional pain theories based in part on observations that the correlation between pain and physical damage is sometimes poor. Anecdotal examples include traumatic injuries (in which pain is sometimes absent) and the "phantom limb" syndrome (in which pain sensations are sometimes experienced in parts of the body that have been amputated). Medical understanding of pain shifted radically with the introduction of Melzack and Wall's "gate control" theory (Melzack and Wall, 1965). That theory involved an attempt to explain the observed properties of pain, including psychological modulation of pain experiences, by reference to human neuroanatomy. In essence, the theory suggested that the experience of pain is synthesized from (1) sensory information from multiple ascending nerve pathways in the spinal cord and (2) modulating signals that descend from the cerebral cortex and thalamus (brain). Ultimately, pain experience was attributed to the complex integration of ascending and descending nervous impulses in

---

[2] In the previous chapter, we discussed how pain is assessed in the California system to determine disability ratings.

[3] Reportedly, this theory was first formalized by the philosopher Rene Descartes in the 17th century. See Melzack (1999b).

[4] See, e.g., American Medical Association, (2000, pp. 568–569).

the dorsal horn region of the spinal cord. The gate control theory of pain generated a great deal of empirical work and debate, and it represented a significant step forward in elucidating the contribution of dynamic brain processes (including psychological processes) to the physical mechanisms of pain (Melzack, 1999b, note 5).

Although the gate control theory offers a neurological basis for the influence of psychological factors in mediating pain experiences, that theory does not fully address the problem of chronic pain in the absence of physical damage. Recent medical scholarship on the subject of pain has acknowledged that even when pain sensations originate from a physical pathology, those sensations can sometimes become independent of the pathology that gave rise to them (American Medical Association, 2000, pp. 567–568). The premise is that physical damage generates a set of pain signals in the nervous system, and those signals may sometimes lead to self-sustaining alterations in underlying neural pain mechanisms. Melzack (1999b) formalized some of these notions in a new "neuromatrix" theory of pain, postulating that pain is a "multidimensional experience produced by characteristic neurosignature patterns of nerve impulses, generated by a widely distributed neural network . . . in the brain" (Melzack, 1999a). The central tenet of the neuromatrix theory is that the experience of pain sensation is ultimately synthesized by brain neural mechanisms. Although those brain mechanisms are influenced by, and receive input from, sensory receptors throughout the body, the mechanisms may be sufficient by themselves to produce pain experiences (as in the phantom limb syndrome). Psychological factors may also influence pain experiences through the medium of the same brain mechanisms (i.e., the neuromatrix). Melzack and others have undertaken at least some empirical work to identify specific neural structures involved in generating pain sensations, consistent with the neuromatrix theory (Melzack, 1999a).

In sum, the current understanding of pain has moved away from the belief that pain is directly correlated with physical harm. Instead, researchers have focused on understanding the role of the central nervous system and brain processes in mediating and integrating pain sensations. It has long been observed that pain sometimes occurs in the absence of physical harm, and that physical harm sometimes does not give rise to pain. These anecdotal observations have supported the development of new pain theories, suggesting (1) that psychological factors can influence pain sensation through the medium of brain neural mechanisms, and (2) that patterns of neural signals that give rise to pain may, in some instances, become independent of the initial physical pathologies that gave rise to them. Despite these theories and related empirical research, clinical medicine nevertheless continues to struggle to understand the manifestation of pain in connection with various forms of disease and injury. Chronic back pain, for example, is the cause of a significant fraction of workers' compensation claims that in some instances have identifiable physical precursors but in other instances lack them.[5] Consequently, medical assessment for pain-related disability tends to draw a distinction between pain associated with known physical pathology and pain for which a physical cause cannot be identified. As is discussed in the next section, this distinction is imperfect, and likely leads to cases in which significant subjective judgment must be exercised on the part of physician-evaluators.

Methods of Pain Assessment

Researchers have developed a number of different formal systems for assessing pain.[6] We should note, however, that the evaluation of pain-related disability for workers' compensation presents some issues distinct from those surrounding pain assessment in general. While pain assessment may be more or less focused on quantifying the intensity of the pain experience or describing the quality of pain sensations, assessment for workers' compensation requires several additional considerations. First, an evaluation for workers' compensation needs to focus not only on the pain itself, but also on the nature and extent of the functional disability that derives from it. Second, for a disability to be compensable, that disability must be caused by a workplace exposure or injury. By implication, when pain causes disability, the pain itself must derive from workplace exposure or injury. Third, in many instances, the putative connection between pain and workplace injury would presumably be reflected by an underlying, identifiable physical pathology. Absent that, evaluation questions may arise in regard to whether pain is psychiatric in its origin (which may necessitate a different level of work causality for compensability under workers' compensation), or whether observed pain can reliably be tied to workplace exposure at all. This issue will only become more important given the new requirement to apportion compensation of permanent disability to the level of workplace causation, which was introduced by SB 899.

What follows is a discussion of pain-related disability assessment guidelines (1) as formulated by the AMA and (2) as elucidated in the Neuromusculoskeletal Evaluation Guidelines of the California IMC. As will become clear, these guidelines require substantial subjective judgment in the conduct of assessments by physicians. Although recent theoretical models of pain have moved away from drawing hard distinctions between physical and psychogenic pain mechanisms, those models have not been integrated into assessment guidelines for evaluating pain-related disability.

The *AMA Guides* consist of a series of chapters focusing on the assessment of impairment in various organ systems and parts of the body. Notably, psychiatric ill-

---

[5] See the discussions in Flor and Turk (1984) and Turk and Flor (1984).

[6] For example, see the discussion in Institute of Medicine (1987, pp. 211–231) and Turk and Melzack (1992).

ness and pain are the subjects of separate chapters. In discussing the assessment of pain, the *AMA Guides* state, as a threshold matter, that physicians are sharply divided between those who tend to view controversial pain syndromes as behavioral in origin and those who favor biological explanations even when unsupported by medical research. Correspondingly, the AMA indicates that its pain assessment algorithm is to be used only in evaluating (1) excess pain associated with verifiable medical conditions[7] or (2) well-established pain syndromes without significant, identifiable organ dysfunction.[8] With regard to the latter, the AMA provides an illustrative list of "well-established" pain syndromes, which includes headache, posttherapeutic neuralgia, tic douloureux, erythromelalgia, and reflex sympathetic dystrophy. The *AMA Guides* draw a distinction between these sorts of conditions and other ambiguous or controversial pain syndromes that are deemed formally "unratable." Given that the list of illustrative "well-established" conditions is open-ended, it seems likely that subjective physician judgment is involved in deciding how the *AMA Guides* apply to individual cases.

Under the *AMA Guides*' rating procedures, an evaluating physician begins by conducting an informal pain assessment. Where mild pain results in a small incremental impairment beyond that attributable to objective physical dysfunction, the evaluator is instructed simply to increase the physical impairment rating by up to 3 percent. Where informal assessment suggests that pain impairment is more substantial, however, then the AMA requires that a formal assessment be undertaken. Formal pain assessment under the *AMA Guides* focuses on pain severity, related activity restrictions, emotional distress, and "pain behaviors" (i.e., characteristic patterns of communication that either exaggerate or minimize the apparent effects of pain on ADLs). The AMA provides quantitative scales for scoring the first three of these four dimensions of pain assessment and more open-ended guidelines for assessing pain behaviors.[9] Formal assessment also calls for a finding that the subject has achieved maximal medical improvement in reducing his or her pain (based on treatment history), as well as a clinical judgment in regard to that person's credibility. Ultimately, the *AMA Guides* provide an algorithm for combining these various ratings into a single score (on a scale of 0–80), which is then used for formal classification of pain-related impairment into one of four categories: mild, moderate, moderately severe, and severe. The AMA does not offer any empirical validation for its rating scales

---

[7] Note that "excess" pain refers to pain causing severe deficits in activities of daily living (ADLs), beyond the impairment rating that derives from the physical injury itself. See American Medical Association (2000, p. 570).

[8] The *AMA Guides* also refer to "associated pain syndromes"—a third category of ratable pain, which is similar in its application to the first two categories. See American Medical Association (2000, p. 570).

[9] Oddly, the AMA presents its own scales as one method, but not the only method, for assessing these dimensions in a formal pain evaluation. Consequently, there is ambiguity regarding what other scales or methods might be acceptable alternatives under the *AMA Guides*.

or its classification scheme. Ultimately, there appear to be several elements in the *AMA Guides'* assessment protocol for which ambiguous standards or subjective judgments may cloud the findings from an evaluation.

Under the Neuromusculoskeletal Evaluation Guidelines of the California IMC, the criteria for evaluating pain are, however, more ambiguous. Formal assessment of pain under the IMC guidelines is one element of a larger evaluation protocol that also addresses objective evidence of organic impairment and legal thresholds for causation, stationary status, apportionment, and other factors that affect compensation under workers' compensation. Pain assessment under the IMC guidelines is subsumed by the heading "subjective factors of disability," and the IMC guidelines cross-reference Section 9727 of Title 8 of the California Code of Regulations, defining "ratable terminology" for subjective complaints of pain.

In essence, the IMC guidelines require classification of the severity of pain into one of four categories (mild, slight, moderate, or severe), based on the extent to which pain causes a handicap in the performance of activities that precipitate the pain. The IMC guidelines also require a rating of the frequency of complaints of pain into one of four categories (occasional, intermittent, frequent, and constant). Finally, in addition to these ratings, the IMC guidelines suggest including an evaluative description of (1) those activities that give rise to pain, (2) the intensity and duration of pain complaints, (3) activities precluded by the complaints, and (4) the means necessary for relief of pain. The IMC guidelines do not specify any more detailed methodology for how these various ratings and descriptions should be undertaken. Nor do the guidelines include citations to empirical evidence in support of this evaluation procedure or any background information regarding how the procedure was derived. Notably, the IMC guidelines do require an explanation from the evaluator where "work restrictions based on subjective factors . . . are out of proportion to objective findings [of physical injury]."

Final Points on the Challenges in Assessing Pain

The assessment of pain-related disability for purposes of workers' compensation shares many of the same difficulties as other sorts of workers' compensation assessments. Beyond simply evaluating pain-related functional impairment, clinicians are also required to develop opinions regarding workplace causation of impairment and apportionment of impairment to industrial and non-industrial factors. These kinds of judgments call not only for the application of legal standards that are otherwise outside the traditional domain of medicine but also for implicit comparisons with pain-related impairment as it might have existed in a world in which a workplace injury or exposure never took place. Such judgments are in some instances fundamentally speculative, even with regard to disability cases for which objective physical damage is clearly evident. Moreover, the assessment of chronic pain injects additional complexity into the workers' compensation evaluation process, because pain-related functional impairment by definition goes beyond that which can be accounted for by observable physical pathology. Thus, assessing pain for workers' compensation presents many of the same challenges as other workers' compensation assessments, compounded by the subjective quality of the pain experienced by individual claimants and the subjective judgments of clinical evaluators in determining the syndromal basis, causation, and apportionment of pain.

A number of empirical technologies and instruments can be used to quantify various aspects of pain sensation and experience. At least some of these instruments possess well-known psychometric properties, including reasonable reliability and evidence of convergent validity (the ability to demonstrate that things that should be related really are) (American Medical Association, 2000). However, pain itself is fundamentally a subjective personal experience. Consequently, evaluations of pain necessarily entail self-reported data on the nature of that subjective experience, or otherwise require a focus on independently observable behaviors that can be attributed to pain. Neither of these sorts of assessment methods addresses the underlying question of whether pain complaints are "real" (i.e., biologically mediated) or are "merely" psychological, and current theories of pain suggest that the distinction may be less meaningful than it was once thought to be.

For purposes of workers' compensation clinical evaluations, the challenge for medical examiners is to undertake a meaningful and reliable assessment of pain-related disability, given the significant ambiguities in legal and procedural standards for doing so. For workers' compensation policymakers, by contrast, the challenge is to determine the extent to which subjective pain experience, independent of underlying physical pathology, falls within the scope of injury that workers' compensation is intended to address and is capable of addressing. With SB 899, policymakers in California appeared to be interested in moving toward a system of disability evaluation that relies more on observable, and presumably "objective," medical evidence of disability. This chapter highlights the fact that relying exclusively on observable, physical harm may necessarily exclude a number of legitimately disabling workplace injuries. Moreover, while the standards in the *AMA Guides* likely involve less subjectivity on the part of physicians than the standards in the IMC guidelines, even with the *AMA Guides* some subjectivity remains.

CHAPTER FIVE

Evaluation of Targeting of Disability Ratings in California

In this chapter, we evaluate the performance of the California permanent partial disability rating schedule with regard to the targeting of disability ratings. The key feature of the California rating system is that it is designed to convert all the relevant information about a disability—specifically, the severity of impairment, age, and occupation—into a single quantitative measure. For this system to achieve horizontal and vertical equity (see Chapter Two), it must systematically assign higher ratings to more severely disabled workers both within and between different types of impairments. We refer to this assignment as the proper *targeting of disability ratings* because, for a given wage, higher disability ratings necessarily imply higher disability benefits.

In the past, disability-rating systems have lacked an empirical basis to support the ranking of impairments. The California system is based on what are essentially best guesses as to how various impairments will limit people of various ages from performing in certain occupations. Berkowitz and Burton (1987) demonstrated how earnings losses, which essentially provide an independent measure of disability, could be used to track the performance of disability ratings. More recently, Peterson et al. (1997) and Reville et al. (2002a) used estimated earnings losses for large samples of California workers to evaluate the performance of California's rating schedule. The basic idea is straightforward: If earnings losses and disability ratings both accurately reflect the extent to which an individual is disabled and unable to work (or limited in the ability to work), then we would expect earnings losses and disability ratings to be highly correlated with each other.

Our methods for measuring the economic outcomes of disabling injuries and our analyses that are described in this chapter are worth examining as more than just an evaluation of the pre–SB 899 rating system. The methods we discuss in this chapter form the basis of the revision in ratings that is required in SB 899.

This chapter evaluates the California ratings system by comparing disability ratings to earnings losses, because earnings losses serve as a proxy for the diminished earnings capacity of injured workers. We argue that when the ranking of impairments by ratings differs from the ranking by earnings losses, then the system is not equitable. The solution can be to revise the relative ranking of impairments using empirical data on loss of earnings capacity. This appears to be the approach that was mandated by SB 899.

Past studies have provided mixed evidence about the extent to which the California system targets benefits appropriately. Peterson et al. (1997) found only a small correlation between disability ratings and earnings losses. In particular, they found that even very-low-rated claims were associated with substantial long-term earnings losses. For example, workers with injuries having a disability rating of 1–5 percent experienced three-year proportional earnings losses of 28.5 percent on average. However, these results were based on ratings from the California Workers' Compensation Insurance Rating Bureau (WCIRB), which are estimated ratings by claims adjusters (often made early in the life of a claim) submitted for the purposes of setting reserves (for future liabilities against a claim). These ratings likely do not include all the medical information used by the California Disability Evaluation Unit (DEU) to compute disability ratings and may not represent the final disability ratings. Peterson et al. (1997) matched WCIRB ratings to DEU ratings and showed that the WCIRB ratings often differed substantially from associated DEU ratings.

By using data on estimated earnings losses matched to DEU ratings, Reville et al. (2002a) provided somewhat more encouraging evidence on the California system's performance in targeting benefits. Focusing on upper-extremity musculoskeletal impairments, they found a closer correlation between the proportional earnings losses and disability ratings of injured workers than did Peterson et al. (1997). In particular, the claims with disability ratings of 1–5 percent had proportional earnings losses of close to 5 percent.

But while the Reville et al. (2002a) results were more promising than the Peterson et al. results with regard to vertical equity, they raised serious questions about horizontal equity. Unlike the earlier RAND study, Reville et al. evaluated the targeting of benefits for different types of impairment, specifically impairments to the shoulder, elbow, and wrist. They found significant differences in average earnings losses for different impairments with similar ratings. For instance, impairments to the shoulder tended to have higher proportional earnings losses for a given disability rating, particularly for claims with ratings of 10–25 percent. By comparison, impairments to the elbow had relatively low earnings loss for a given rating, and Reville et al. found little difference in earnings losses for cases with a 10 percent rating and cases with a 20 percent rating. Moreover, using a Chi-square test, they rejected the null hypothesis of equal losses for the different impairment types, with a p-value of less than 0.01 for seven of the ten specific disability ratings they tested. These results were generally consistent with the results of Berkowitz and Burton (1987).[1]

---

[1] Park and Butler (2000) used a similar methodology to evaluate impairment ratings in Minnesota and found that impairment ratings do a poor job of predicting earnings losses. That study is limited, however, because Park and Butler lacked a suitable group of control workers with which to estimate earnings losses and were forced to

The analysis in this report builds on the analysis in Reville et al. (2002a) in a number of important ways. First, we consider a much larger range of impairment categories and expand the analysis of vertical and horizontal equity to a more representative sample of permanent disabilities in California. In addition, while the analysis of the earlier study focused on the *standard disability rating* (the rating based solely on physician evaluation of disability severity, before adjustments for age, occupation, and subjective criteria), we extended the analysis to examine the performance of the *final rating,* the rating including all adjustments for age and occupation.

Data and Methods

In this section, we describe our data on disability ratings and earnings and outline our approach to measuring the economic outcomes of disabling injuries. Our goal is to evaluate the targeting of benefits by comparing injury severity across various impairments using labor market outcomes. We measure economic outcomes using the methodology developed in, among other studies, Peterson et al. (1997), Reville (1999), Reville et al. (2001b), Reville and Schoeni (2001), and Reville et al. (2002b).

Measuring Losses from Injury
We illustrate our approach to estimating earnings losses in Figure 5.1, which represents hypothetical losses from a permanently disabling workplace injury. The dashed line represents potential earnings for an uninjured worker—the earnings the worker would have received if the injury had not occurred. Potential earnings increase over time, representing the increased earnings associated with increasing experience in the labor market or increasing tenure at the employer. The solid lines represent the observed earnings of the injured worker. After the time of injury, the worker receives no earnings for some period while recovering from the injury. This is the period during which workers' compensation temporary disability benefits are received.

At some point, the worker represented by Figure 5.1 returns to work, perhaps in some modified capacity. The worker returns at a wage that is lower than what he or she received prior to injury. We then observe the worker's wages increasing over time and converging toward the wages the worker would have received had he or she not been injured. This convergence represents *recovery.* However, in this example, we do not observe full wage recovery, and, at the end of the observed period, the worker makes more than he or she made prior to injury but not as much as what he or she would have made if the injury had not happened.

---

use pre-injury wages. As is discussed later in this chapter, there are several important reasons why pre-injury wages are not ideal for estimating earnings losses.

Figure 5.1
Hypothetical Effect on Earnings After a Workplace Injury

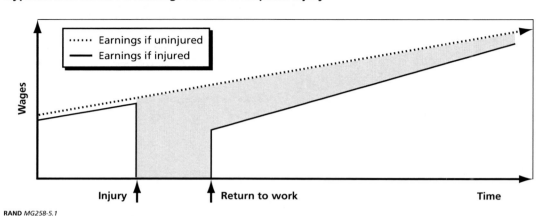

The shaded area in the figure represents the total lost earnings over the period of time after the injury. Estimating the size of this area and comparing earnings losses to disability ratings and verifying whether or not they are positively related are the goals of this analysis. Whereas wages received while the claimant is injured (the solid lines in Figure 5.1) are readily observable with appropriate data, the challenge in estimating earnings losses lies in estimating the uninjured earnings, which are represented by the dotted line.

Pre-injury wage is not a satisfactory proxy for future earnings, particularly when estimating the long-term consequences of permanent disabilities. First, without the injury, the worker may have experienced wage growth over time, which the pre-injury earnings will not measure. Figure 5.1 illustrates that while the injured worker soon exceeds pre-injury earnings, his or her earnings nevertheless fall below what he or she would have earned had the injury never occurred. Second, if the injury had not occurred, it is possible that the injured worker would have been unemployed or exited the workforce for various reasons. It cannot be assumed that the injured worker would have earned the equivalent of the pre-injury earnings in every post-injury earnings period.

Using Matched Uninjured Coworkers as a Control Group

For the reasons stated above, instead of using pre-injury earnings, we estimate uninjured earnings in the post-injury period using the earnings of a quasi-experimental comparison (control) group. This approach draws its inspiration from the literature on training-program evaluations (e.g., Dehejia and Wahba, 1999; Heckman and Hotz, 1989; Holland, 1986; and Lalonde, 1986). The control group consists of workers who were similar to the injured workers with respect to demographic and economic characteristics, but who did not experience a workplace injury during the time period under examination.

For the comparison group, we selected up to five workers at the same firm who had earnings that were closest to the injured worker's over the year prior to injury. The comparison workers were also required to have similar tenure, where tenure is measured using three levels: less than or equal to one year on the job, one to two years on the job, or more than two years on the job. In each quarter after injury, we calculated the difference between the injured worker's earnings and the average earnings of the worker's comparison group. This gave us the estimate of earnings loss in that quarter. We repeated this calculation also for quarters prior to the injury in order to test the quality of the match. We describe this approach formally in the following paragraphs.

Let y_t^I represent the injured worker's earnings (where I denotes "injured" and the subscript t denotes "time from the injury").

Let y_t^U represent the comparison worker's earnings (where U denotes "uninjured").

We estimated y_t^U using the average earnings of the n comparison workers for that individual injured worker, where n is between 1 and 5, depending upon the number of available comparable uninjured workers at the injured worker's employer.

For any injured worker, the undiscounted earnings loss between the time of injury, which we denoted as $t=0$, and some future date, T, is shown in Equation 1:

$$\text{earnings loss} = \sum_{t=0}^{T} (y_t^U - y_t^I) \qquad (1)$$

Usually, when we report earnings losses, we report the average of the quantity in Equation 1 across all injured workers.

In many cases, we were interested in estimating proportional earnings losses, or that fraction of potential "uninjured" earnings over a period of time that an injured worker experiences earnings losses. Normalizing earnings losses by what the individual would have made facilitates comparison over time when average earnings may be growing. It also allows comparison across firms that have different average earnings, such as firms in different industries or different states. Proportional earnings losses are estimated as earnings losses divided by the total earnings received by the comparison group, as shown in Equation 2:

$$\text{proportional earnings loss} = \frac{\displaystyle\sum_{t=0}^{T}(y_t^U - y_t^I)}{\displaystyle\sum_{t=0}^{T}(y_t^U)} \tag{2}$$

Note that while we describe the earnings loss here without discounting to reflect the present value of losses, we actually compute earnings losses using quarterly discounting, as described in Reville (1999).

Linked Administrative Data

Our data in this study are similar to the data in Peterson et al. (1997). Workers' compensation claims data are linked to earnings data for claimants based on their Social Security number, and this information is combined with earnings data to identify the control group. While the 1997 study used workers' compensation data from the WCIRB, this study uses a sample of ratings from the California DEU.

The State of California's DEU performs between 60,000 and 80,000 ratings of permanent disabilities each year. The dataset used here was drawn from evaluations done on injuries occurring between January 1, 1991, and December 31, 1997. This sample resulted in a total of 416,269 evaluations of permanent impairments.[2] The DEU data contain specific information about the type of impairment and severity of the impairment, and important demographic data (gender, age at injury, average weekly wage at injury, address, and occupation).

The earnings data are from the Base Wage file maintained by the California Employment Development Department (EDD). Every quarter, employers covered by unemployment insurance (UI) in California are required to report the quarterly earnings of every employee to the EDD. These reports are stored in the Base Wage file. The industries covered by UI are virtually identical to the industries covered by workers' compensation; therefore, a worker injured at a firm against which he or she can make a workers' compensation claim should also have a record for that quarter in the Base Wage file. With roughly 95 percent of employees in California covered by the UI system, the matched DEU-EDD data provide a substantially complete and accurate California quarterly earnings history for permanent disability claimants. We have all the available data for every worker in California covered by UI from the first quarter of 1991 through the first quarter of 1999.[3]

---

[2] A large majority of these evaluations involves separate individuals; less than 5 percent of all cases in our database involve individuals with multiple PPD claims.

[3] Data are not available in every year for every worker that we observe at the time of injury. In some cases, injured or comparison workers drop out of the sample, and we do not know if they left the state or stopped working for some reason. This issue is discussed in greater detail in Reville and Schoeni (2001).

After dropping claims without individual identifiers or information on disability type, or that occurred after April 1, 1997, we ended up with 346,960 claims. For more than 69 percent of injured workers in the DEU system, we were able to find data in the EDD files on workers employed in the same firm at the quarter of injury and in the same tenure category who had quarterly earnings within 10 percent of the injured worker's earnings over the four quarters prior to injury. Claims for which this match was not possible were dropped from the analysis.[4] Thus, we are able to create a database that includes the type of impairment, disability rating, and the estimated earnings losses for 241,685 PPD claimants in California injured from January 1, 1991, to April 1, 1997. Of these records, 192,682 have data on earnings losses three years after injury, which will be the focus of our analysis.

Most of the ratings in the DEU data, which are for about 65 percent of all claims, are based on medical reports completed by "neutral" doctors selected to perform comprehensive ratings, called *summary ratings,* while others are based on reports completed by doctors selected by an applicant (i.e., a claimant) or a defense attorney as part of litigation; we call the latter ratings *applicant ratings* and *defense ratings*, respectively. In this section, we restrict our analysis to summary ratings. We consider applicant and defense ratings in Chapter Seven, where we evaluate the consistency of disability ratings.

A final distinction that we make in this analysis is between single-disability and multiple-disability claims. Most of the ratings in our database, approximately 85 percent of the summary ratings, claim a single impairment suffered by an injured worker. Note that in the California system "multiple disabilities" refers to impairments to "separate members or organs of the body" (see Division of Workers' Compensation, 1997). This definition rules out cases with different impairments in the same body part or cases with separate impairments in what are called "bilateral disabilities," such as disabilities in both legs. Multiple disabilities are rated according to a complicated schedule to ensure that the final rating does not exceed 100 percent.[5] For most of our analysis, we focus on single disabilities, but we provide some general results for the most common pairings of multiple disabilities.[6]

---

[4] The primary reason for not finding a match was that workers in smaller firms were less likely to have a coworker with earnings in the allowed wage range. This factor will lead to a sample that overrepresents workers at larger firms. For more information on the impact of firm size on estimates of wage loss, see Reville and Schoeni (2001). In Appendix B, we argue that firm size should have little impact on the observed relationship between earnings losses and disability ratings, so this oversampling is not of great concern for the results reported here.

[5] Consider the case of a worker with impairments to two separate extremities, the more severe with a rating of A and the less severe with a rating of B. The final rating is given by the formula $A + (100 - A) \times B + B/10$, which is capped at 100 percent. Successive disabilities are rated according to the same formula, with the combined rating acting as disability A and the successive disability acting as disability B.

[6] In practice, we do observe in the sample some cases that claim multiple disabilities to the same body part (or at least a family of body parts). Such cases could reflect measurement error in the data or confusion by raters or physicians over the correct way to rate disabilities.

Because the quality of the match between injured workers and control workers is crucial for the estimation of earnings losses, we conclude this section with an evaluation of the matching procedure. Matching on income occurs for earnings reported during the four quarters prior to the injury. Therefore, if the control group is of high quality, the income of the injured worker should approximately equal the income of the comparison workers during a reasonable period of time prior to the match. Figure 5.2 displays relative earnings, or the percentage of average earnings of the injured worker relative to the average earnings of the comparison workers, in the three years (12 quarters) prior to injury and the three years after injury (so that 100 percent is equal to earnings for the injured worker and his or her control group). Quarter 0 denotes the quarter of injury.

By examining the closeness of earnings for injured workers and the control workers in the quarters prior to injury, we can assess the quality of the match. For each injured worker in the merged data set, we calculate income relative to the average incomes of the workers' matched controls (see Equation 1). We do this for 12 quarters before the injury and for 12 quarters after the injury. Injured workers and their controls are required to match wages only in the average of the four quarters before injury, not in the eight quarters prior to injury.

Figure 5.2
Earnings of Injured Workers Relative to Control Workers, by Quarters After Injury

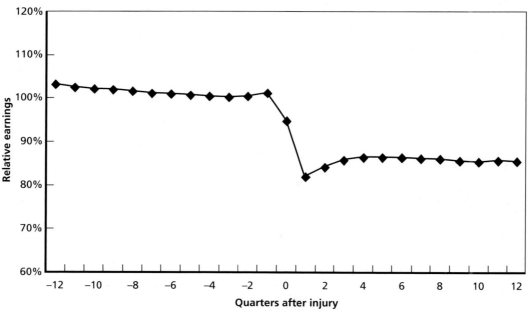

Comparing the incomes of the injured and control workers in the fifth through 12th quarter prior to an injury allows us to test the adequacy of our control groups. If the wages of injured workers and their controls differed radically prior to the matching period, this would imply that these two groups of workers differ in unobserved ways, and that the controls are of poor quality. However, Figure 5.2 shows that the injured workers' wages are very close to 100 percent of the control workers' wages (i.e., they are very close to being equal) for the entire three years prior to injury. We conclude that, based on the evidence regarding wages in the quarters prior to injury, our approach of selecting comparison workers yields high-quality matches. Longer periods of pre-injury earnings have been examined, and the quality of the matching approach has been preserved (see Peterson et al., 1997; Reville, 1999; and Reville and Schoeni, 2001).

As a final point, the data used to produce Figure 5.2 included only single-injury claims with a standard rating. Because of attrition by workers in and out of the sample, not all quarters have the same sample sizes, but in no quarter do we have fewer than 70,000 observations. In general, the overall match quality remains high when the sample is broken up by injury type or by other control variables.

Results

We began our analysis by studying the overall performance of the California rating schedule in assigning higher ratings to workers with higher earnings losses. This gave us an indication of how well the system performs in terms of vertical equity. We then addressed the issue of horizontal equity by examining whether workers with different types of impairments, but similar earnings losses, receive similar disability ratings. In this section, we consider both single-disability and multiple-disability cases. We conclude this chapter with a discussion of a portion of the post–SB 899 reform of the rating system: the reordering of the California rating system based on earnings losses.

The analysis in this chapter assumes that when higher earnings losses are associated with higher disability ratings, it is because the ratings predicted the losses, rather than caused them. In Appendix B, we discuss the possibility that higher ratings cause higher earnings losses (through the effect of higher benefits on the supply of labor). If higher ratings caused higher wage losses, that reverse causation would invalidate the evaluation approach. We do not, however, find much evidence for this effect.

Earnings Losses by Disability Rating

We begin by comparing earnings losses to broad ranges of disability ratings, with the results reported in Figure 5.3. On the figure's horizontal axis, we indicate whether

Figure 5.3
Three-Year Cumulative Proportional Earnings Losses by Disability Rating Group

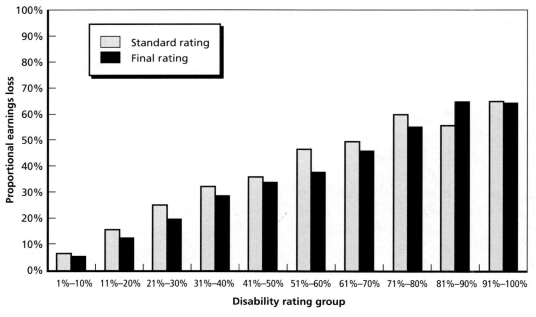

the disability rating fell between 1 and 10 percent, 11 and 20 percent, and so forth, up to the highest range of 91 to 100 percent.[7] On the vertical axis of the figure, we display the average three-year (12 quarters) cumulative proportional earnings loss percentages for cases in each ratings range. We focus on three-year losses because Peterson et al. (1997) and Reville et al. (2001c) show that proportional earnings losses do not appear to change much over longer time periods. Given that the longer the time period we use, the more observations we lose from the sample because of a limited number of years of post-injury earnings, it is convenient to use the shortest post-injury time period for which we feel that earnings losses are reasonably predictive of long-term losses. We consider two types of ratings in the analysis, the unadjusted standard rating and the final rating, taking into account all the various modifiers (the results are identical if we include intermediate ratings that are only partially adjusted).

These results show that, on average, proportional earnings losses increase as both the standard and final ratings increase. Impairments with a standard rating be-

---

[7] These categories assume the ratings necessarily take integer values. For some cases, most notably standard ratings modified by what is called a "range-of-motion" modifier, the ratings may not be integers. So, the 11–20 percent category actually includes any rating strictly greater than 10 percent and less than or equal to 20 percent.

tween 1 and 10 percent have proportional earnings losses of approximately 6 percent. Those with a standard rating from 41 to 50 percent have proportional earnings losses of approximately 36 percent. Impairments with the highest standard ratings, between 91 and 100 percent, have proportional earnings losses equal to approximately 64 percent on average. More generally, every group of impairments with higher standard ratings has higher proportional earnings losses, except the standard ratings of 71 to 80 percent (which have proportional earnings losses of 59.3 percent on average) and those from 81 to 90 percent (which have average losses of approximately 55.4 percent).

Similar results are obtained when we consider the final rating. This is unsurprising, given that adjustments to the standard rating can be positive or negative (e.g., workers younger than 39 have their ratings adjusted downward, and workers older than 39 have theirs adjusted upward). This finding implies that the difference between the standard and final rating is small on average. With final ratings, every group of higher ratings has higher average proportional earnings losses than all lower-rated groups, except the 91–100 percent rating group, which has losses that are virtually identical.

The implication of Figure 5.3 is that the California rating schedule does a reasonable job of targeting higher ratings, and therefore higher benefits, toward injured workers who are more severely disabled. However, the figure masks considerable heterogeneity in sample sizes within each rating group. There are 68,295 cases that have a summary rating, are single-disability, have a final rating, and for which we were able to compute proportional earnings losses 12 quarters after injury.[8] Figure 5.4 illustrates the distribution of these ratings. The figure shows that a large majority of ratings are relatively small: About 18 percent have a final rating between 1 and 5 percent, while approximately 39 percent have a rating less than 10 percent. Approximately 84 percent of all cases have a final rating below 40 percent.

To ensure that the smooth aggregate picture presented in Figure 5.3 does not mask substantial variability within rating categories, we need to consider a more disaggregated picture.

Figure 5.5 illustrates the average three-year cumulative proportional earnings losses for each single digit of disability ratings for ratings between 1 and 35 percent. Here, we focus on only the final disability rating. The dotted lines above and below the line relating disability ratings to earnings losses represent the 95 percent confidence interval for the earnings losses.

---

[8] While all observations have a standard rating, there are many observations (approximately one-third) in which the final rating is missing. Nevertheless, as suggested by Figure 5.3, the two ratings are similar enough on average that our qualitative results are essentially identical if we use the standard rating.

Figure 5.4
Distribution of Final Disability Ratings in the Matched Sample

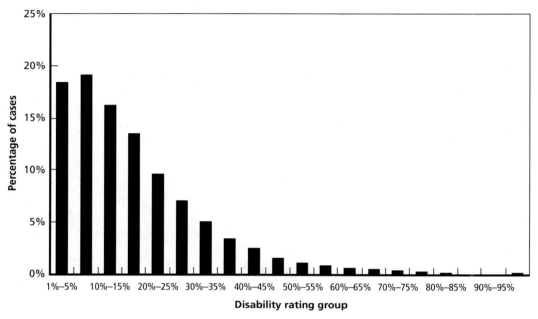

From Figure 5.5, we see that even when focusing on a very disaggregated picture, the average earnings losses bear a fairly strong positive correlation with the disability ratings. The proportional losses in cases with ratings from 1 to 5 percent are highly variable but are quite small (close to or below 5 percent) on average. The average proportional losses increase fairly steadily with the ratings, with ratings of 10 percent having losses equal to 9.2 percent on average, ratings of 25 percent having losses of about 19.3 percent on average, and ratings of 35 percent having losses of 26 percent on average. We can see from the figure that the confidence intervals around the average losses are fairly tight, indicating a clear positive correlation between ratings and losses. However, it is important to note that the correlation between ratings and losses holds only in the aggregate. For any two ratings, there are a number of cases in which there is little difference in average earnings losses, or earnings losses may be lower for the higher rating. One could use this finding to argue that assigning identical benefits to ratings that fall within five- or ten-point intervals could lead to improved vertical equity over the assignment of benefits to ratings on a continuous level (i.e., each additional rating point provides higher benefits) that currently exists, although such a system would inevitably raise questions of equity for those just above or below the rating-group thresholds.

Figure 5.5
Three-Year Earnings Losses by Final Disability Rating

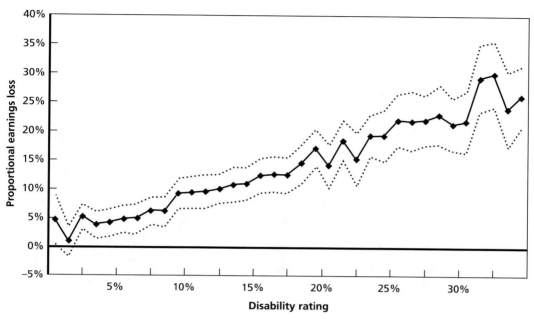

   While our focus until now has been on single-disability claims, we are also in-terested in the California schedule's ability to target higher ratings toward more se-vere multiple disabilities. To do so, we compared the final rating of single-disability claims to that of claims with two disabilities.[9] We once again focused on average three-year cumulative losses, using rating groups from 1 to 10 percent, 11 to 20 per-cent, and so on. The results of this analysis are displayed in Figure 5.6.

   Figure 5.6 shows that ratings for multiple-disability claims increase with higher proportional earnings losses, such as what occurs for single-disability ratings. More-over, the relationship between ratings and earnings losses are fairly similar for the single-disability and multiple-disability claims. For the lower-rated claims, in par-ticular, the average proportional earnings losses for the multiple-disability claims are almost identical to the losses for the single-disability claims. There are some differ-ences in the higher-rated claims, particularly for claims with ratings between 81 and 90 percent. Over this range, single-disability claims have average losses of about 64 percent, while the multiple-disability claims have average losses of about 50 percent.

---

[9] Recall that single-disability claims can involve more than one impairment, but to only the one body part (or family of body parts).

Figure 5.6
Three-Year Earnings Losses for Single- and Multiple-Disability Cases by Rating Group

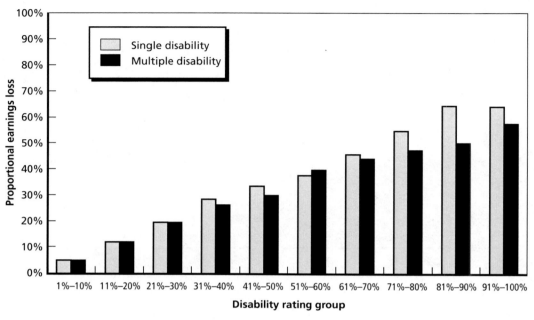

RAND *MG258-5.6*

As we mentioned earlier, however, the sample sizes at the higher ratings are fairly small, and the difference between losses for multiple- and single-disability claims in that rating group is not statistically different from zero.[10]

Overall, our results suggest that the California rating schedule does a good job of ranking disabilities in terms of vertical equity, at least in the aggregate. That is, impairments that receive higher disability ratings on average also have higher observed earnings losses. This holds for even very small (one-point) differences in ratings, and a similar relationship seems to apply to multiple- and single-disability claims.

Earnings Losses by Disability Rating for Different Types of Injuries

The results that we have discussed to this point suggest that the California disability rating schedule targets higher benefits to more severely injured workers on average. While this is informative, it is still possible to have a system that targets benefits ef-

_____

[10] In our database, there are 144 multiple-disability claims and 115 single-disability claims with final ratings between 81 and 90 percent. The average proportional loss in this range for the multiple-disability claims is approximately 0.5, with a standard deviation of approximately 0.898. For the single-disability claims, the average proportional loss is approximately 0.642, with a standard deviation of 0.895. Using this information, we compute a t-statistic of approximately 1.19 for the one-sided test of the hypothesis that earnings losses are higher for the single-disability claims, so we fail to reject the null hypothesis of equal proportional losses.

fectively on average but systematically undercompensates or overcompensates particular kinds of injuries. In other words, even if the system performs well in terms of vertical equity, it might still fail in terms of horizontal equity. In this section, we examine the question of whether or not different kinds of injuries with similar ratings also have similar levels of observed earnings losses. If they do, it would suggest that the system also exhibits an equitable distribution horizontally. If not, it would suggest that ratings may need to be adjusted to improve the equity of the system.

When breaking down workers' compensation claims in California by impairment type, a natural starting place is to focus on impairments to the neck, spine, and pelvis, which from now on we refer to simply as "back impairments." Claims for injuries to the back are by far the most frequently occurring claims in the workers' compensation system, accounting for more than 36 percent of all summary-rated, single-disability PPD claims. In Figure 5.7, we illustrate whether the rating schedule targets higher benefits to back impairments with higher levels of measured severity.

The solid black line in Figure 5.7 represents the proportional losses from back impairments for each disability rating, the dotted lines represent the 95 percent confidence interval, and the gray shaded line represents the earnings losses by disability for all ratings, which is identical to the solid black line in Figure 5.5. From the figure,

Figure 5.7
Three-Year Earnings Losses from Back Impairments by Disability Rating

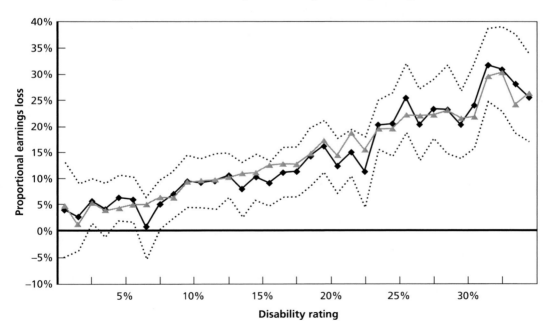

we see that, in general, the proportional losses from back impairments increase fairly steadily with disability ratings. For very-low-rated claims, there seems to be relatively little correlation between ratings and losses, but for claims with disability ratings of 7 percent or higher, there is a clear positive correlation between ratings and losses. One can see that the relationship between losses and ratings for back impairments is very similar to that for all impairments. This finding is perhaps unsurprising, given that injuries to the back account for such a large part of total claims. Nevertheless, it is clear that the general result—that the system targets higher benefits to more-severe disabilities—also holds for back impairments.

While in principle we would like to reproduce this analysis for all major impairment categories, the sample sizes for most categories are too small, and the confidence intervals are too large, to draw meaningful inference for such small partitions of ratings. The results of Reville et al. (2002a) suggest that, in general, upper-extremity injuries exhibit the same positive correlation between earnings losses and disability ratings as back impairments exhibit. However, Reville et al. also found that the very-low-rated claims, in particularly those with ratings under 5 percent, are highly variable and do not always display a clear relationship between ratings and earnings losses.

As a first step toward considering a broader range of impairment categories, we compared earnings losses and disability ratings for four major impairment categories: shoulder impairments (the largest specific upper-extremity impairment), knee impairments (the largest specific lower-extremity impairment), loss of grasping power, and back impairments. Again, we limited the analysis to single-disability, summary-rated cases and considered three-year proportional earnings losses. In this case, we grouped impairments with final ratings of 1–5 percent, 6–10 percent, 11–15 percent, and so on up to 35 percent; all ratings over 35 percent are grouped together. The results of this analysis are presented in Figure 5.8.

Two results are immediately apparent from Figure 5.8. First, the proportional earnings losses for each impairment type increase with the disability rating for almost every ratings range for each impairment type. This finding, again, supports the notion that on average the rating schedule ties higher benefits to more-serious impairments. However, clear disparities also appear to exist among the observed proportional earnings losses of different impairments that are assigned similar ratings.

In the lowest rating range, that with ratings between 1 and 5 percent, back impairments have the highest estimated losses, about 4.6 percent, while knee impairments have the lowest, about 0.9 percent. For all other rating groups, however, shoulder impairments have substantially higher proportional earnings losses than all other types of injury. Knee impairments have the lowest earnings losses on average, although the loss of grasping power seems to have lower losses for the highest rating category.

Figure 5.8
Three-Year Earnings Losses by Disability Rating Category and Impairment Type

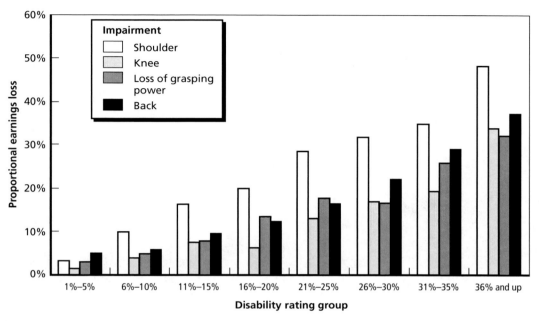

RAND *MG258-5.8*

These results provide a striking illustration of the impact of a lack of empirical bases for rating schedules. It is usually possible to show that between two individuals with the same impairment, one impairment is more severe than the other, and this is why, within impairment types, each rating group has higher proportional wage losses than every lower-rating group. However, it is far more difficult to compare severity across impairments involving different body parts. Moreover, equally severe impairments for different body parts may have different impacts on earnings. Wage losses across rating groups enable us to provide a common standard of comparison.

While this analysis highlights some of the difficulties in assigning disability ratings for different types of impairments, psychiatric impairments are particularly challenging for any rating system. Objective medical information is more difficult to obtain, and translating the medical information that exists into expected loss of ability to compete in the labor market requires information on the occupational implications of psychiatric conditions, which largely does not exist. Claims for psychiatric impairments also involve complex questions of causality that make them controversial in any workers' compensation system. Figure 5.9 demonstrates just how much difficulty the rating system has in dealing with psychiatric impairments. The figure illustrates the relationship between earnings losses and ratings for the same injury

Figure 5.9
Three-Year Earnings Losses by Disability Rating Category and Impairment Type Including Psychiatric

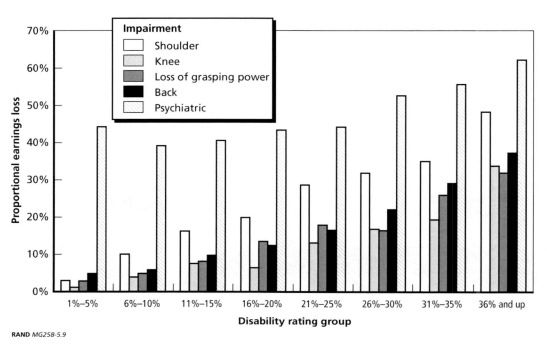

types and rating groups as were illustrated in Figure 5.8, but with the addition of earnings losses for single-impairment psychiatric claims (i.e., those that do not involve a physical injury and are often excluded from compensation in other states' workers' compensation systems). All psychiatric impairment cases, regardless of their rating, have substantial earnings losses, with the average for all rating groups exceeding 38 percent. Low-rated psychiatric impairments have higher earnings losses than many higher-rated psychiatric claims, but the relationship appears weaker than for other impairments. Additionally, every psychiatric rating group has higher losses than all but the highest-rated groups for the other types of impairment.

The five impairment types illustrated in Figure 5.9 account for approximately 66 percent of all single-disability, summary-rated claims. However, the samples for each impairment type shown in these figures vary significantly, particularly for some of the higher-rated groups. There are more than 1,500 cases involving back impairments in each rating group. Shoulder impairments have much smaller sample sizes, with just 147 cases in the 26–30 percent rating group, 83 in the 31–35 percent rating group, and 85 in the 36-percent-and-up rating group. The sample sizes for psychological impairments are even smaller—numbering less than 100 in most of the rating groups and just 28 for the 1–5 percent rating group.

The statistical significance of the differences between earnings losses obviously varies depending on the comparison. Using back impairments as the point of comparison, we can say that the earnings losses for knee impairments are significantly lower than those for back impairments at the 5 percent impairment rating level in three of the seven rating groups. The earnings losses for shoulder impairments are significantly higher statistically than those for back impairments at the 5 percent confidence level for three of the seven groups as well. The earnings losses for loss-of-grasping-power impairments are not statistically significantly different from the earnings losses of back impairments in any of the seven rating groups. Despite the small samples for psychiatric impairments, the earnings losses for psychiatric cases are significantly higher than the losses for back cases at the 5 percent confidence level for all seven ratings categories.

Reordering the Rating Schedule

Our analysis of the California rating schedule suggests that it generally does a better job of ranking the severity of disabilities *within* impairment categories than ranking the severity of disabilities *between* impairment categories. Another way of saying this is that the rating schedule seems to perform relatively well in terms of vertical equity but relatively poorly in terms of horizontal equity. If the basis of the rating is unchanged, it is relatively straightforward to use data on earnings losses to reorder the California rating schedule to improve the horizontal equity.[11] Under SB 899, the reordering appears to be less straightforward, because the basis of the rating is now the *AMA Guides.* In this section, we discuss the reordering of the simple case (the California system) to elucidate the concept, while maintaining a focus on the pre–SB 899 California rating system.

Our data allow us to compute adjustment factors for a number of impairments that are common in California. (Appendix B explains how we derive the adjustment factors.) In Table 5.1, we list the average proportional earnings losses and disability ratings for the 14 impairment categories for which we have 500 observations of summary-rated, single-disability claims. The first column of the table lists the specific impairment type considered. All five of the impairment categories discussed above are listed in the table, along with nine others for which we observed a suitable number of observations. The second column lists the sample size (N) for each impairment type. The third and fourth columns report the average three-year proportional earnings losses and final ratings, respectively, with the standard error of each variable

---

[11] However, it is possible that reordering the benefits to reflect earnings losses could increase the incentives to try to dispute the type of injury. This ties into the issue of the consistency of medical evaluations by physicians, which is discussed in Chapter Seven.

Table 5.1
Earnings Losses and Ratings by Impairment Category: Single Disabilities

Impairment Type	N	Proportional Earnings Losses	Final Rating	Avg.(Rate) / Avg.(WL)
Finger: One digit	1,612	0.019 (0.016)	0.040 (0.001)	2.15
Elbow	2,103	0.066 (0.015)	0.123 (0.002)	1.86
Knee	8,598	0.093 (0.007)	0.170 (0.002)	1.83
Ankle	2,864	0.107 (0.013)	0.170 (0.003)	1.59
Finger: Four digits	899	0.110 (0.026)	0.167 (0.004)	1.52
Loss of grasping power	8,658	0.097 (0.007)	0.143 (0.001)	1.47
Wrist	4,291	0.119 (0.011)	0.161 (0.002)	1.35
Back	23,951	0.163 (0.005)	0.212 (0.001)	1.30
Finger: Five digits	1,788	0.132 (0.019)	0.166 (0.003)	1.26
General upper extremities	6,104	0.182 (0.010)	0.212 (0.002)	1.16
General lower extremities	1,052	0.186 (0.023)	0.215 (0.006)	1.16
Shoulder	5,062	0.123 (0.010)	0.111 (0.001)	0.90
Psychiatric	982	0.495 (0.030)	0.293 (0.007)	0.59
Hearing	1,200	0.217 (0.032)	0.103 (0.003)	0.47

NOTES: Standard errors are shown in parentheses. The table includes all single-disability, summary-rated cases in impairment categories with at least 500 observations. WL = proportional earnings loss.

reported in parentheses. The fifth column lists the ratio of the average final rating to the average earnings losses for each impairment type (i.e., the fourth column divided by the third).

Table 5.1 displays a fairly wide range between the proportional earnings losses and disability ratings of the various impairment types. Impairments to a single finger have average earnings losses of 1.9 percent, which is statistically indistinguishable from zero. The average final rating for these impairments is 4 percent, which is low but still twice as high as the proportional losses. Hearing impairments, by comparison, have average proportional losses of 21.7 percent, but their average disability rating is just 10.3 percent. Psychiatric claims also have low disability ratings relative to their proportional losses, even though they have the highest average ratings by a fairly significant margin. Back injuries, which as we have said are by far the most common impairments, fall fairly close to the middle in terms of the ratio between ratings and losses, ranking eighth in the 14 injuries listed in Table 5.1.

The ratios shown in the fifth column of Table 5.1 are the measures from which we could, in principle, compute adjustments for the various impairments to improve the horizontal equity of the rating system. We could simply choose a baseline impairment category and then divide that impairment type's ratio of ratings to losses by the ratio of all the other impairment types listed in the table. The result would provide us with the appropriate adjustment factor for each type of impairment to equalize the relationship between average ratings and average proportional losses.

While Table 5.1 focuses on single-disability claims, we might also be interested in adjusting the way the rating schedule compensates different multiple-disability claims. In Table 5.2, we compare the average three-year proportional earnings losses and final ratings for eight different pairings of impairments and use these pairings to compute analogous adjustment factors. The variables in this table are the same as those in Table 5.1. In this analysis, we include all summary-rated, two-disability claims with more than 250 observations (we allow for smaller sample sizes, because in general we have fewer multiple-disability claims). Note that all eight groups include an impaired back as part of the claim.

Table 5.2
Earnings Losses and Ratings by Impairment Category: Impairment Pairings

Impairment Group	N	Proportional Earnings Losses	Final Rating	Avg.(Rate) / Avg.(WL)
Back and general lower extremity	280	0.218 (0.048)	0.237 (0.011)	1.09
Back and general upper extremity	1,146	0.223 (0.025)	0.222 (0.005)	1.00
Back and ankle	327	0.225 (0.038)	0.206 (0.009)	0.91
Back and wrist	358	0.204 (0.038)	0.180 (0.007)	0.88
Back and loss of grasping power	1,074	0.196 (0.022)	0.165 (0.004)	0.84
Back and post-traumatic head syndrome (PTHS)	313	0.152 (0.043)	0.127 (0.008)	0.83
Back and knee	973	0.258 (0.024)	0.213 (0.005)	0.83
Back and shoulder	1,483	0.231 (0.018)	0.150 (0.003)	0.65

NOTES: Standard errors are shown in parentheses. The table includes all summary-rated claims with two disabilities and at least 250 observations.

The most noticeable aspect of Table 5.2 is that the average proportional losses for the multiple-disability claims are higher than those for single-disability claims. This finding makes sense, as we would expect a person with more than one impaired body part to be more disabled (i.e., less able to work), all things being equal. The next noteworthy set of results in the table is that the average final ratings are small relative to the average proportional earnings losses. The highest value of the ratio of average disability rating to average proportional losses is 1.09 for the "back and general lower extremity impairments" combination (compared with 2.15 for single-disability claims with one impaired finger). More generally, for 11 of the 14 impairments in Table 5.1, the ratio of average disability rating to average proportional losses is greater than 1, whereas only two of the eight impairment pairs in Table 5.2 have a ratio greater than 1.

Again, we could calculate adjustment factors for the rating system for these impairment pairs by dividing the ratio of average rating to average proportional losses for each by the ratio associated with some baseline impairment. Note that because the final rating is intended to provide the same information across all impairments, we can use the same baseline impairment category for the multiple-disability claims and single-disability claims.

The analysis thus far has assumed that the differences across impairment groups are constant for the same rating. It is possible that the relationship between average ratings and average proportional losses is nonlinear—i.e., the relationship may be different for lower average ratings than for higher average ratings. We address this issue in Appendix B by considering the relationship between these two variables for different quintiles of rating groups. In general, we find that in many cases the relationship does appear to vary across quintiles, but not in any systematic way.

We expect that the relationship between earnings losses and impairment ratings will change over time. This change will occur as the post-injury employment patterns of injured workers improve or deteriorate. It will also occur as medical technology or accommodations for particular disabilities change over time. This observation suggests that a periodic review would be necessary to determine if changes in the adjustment factor might be warranted, as were adopted under SB 899. A periodic revision would provide a means of feedback for the workers' compensation permanent disability system. Over time, equity is maintained, and if return to work improves in California over all, the system could allow for the overall level of benefits to decline.[12] Because the benefits would decline by less than the increase in earnings (because only two-thirds of pre-injury earnings up to a cap are replaced), both injured workers and employers would benefit from such a revision in the system.

---

[12] This assumes that the magnitudes of average ratings were directly tied to data on earnings losses, as opposed to just the relative values of ratings. If data on losses were used only to adjust the relative values without impacting the size of the average rating, then a decline in losses need not have any impact on average benefits.

CHAPTER SIX

Additional Criteria for Adjusting Disability Ratings

In this chapter, we turn our attention to an evaluation of adjustments in the California rating schedule for various factors. As discussed in Chapter Three, one of the primary factors used to adjust disability ratings in California is age. A number of states provide adjustments for age, although not always in the same direction as California. In California, older workers receive higher ratings, whereas in some states, e.g., Colorado, younger workers receive higher ratings. Other states may provide adjustments for age only under certain circumstances; New Mexico, for example, provides higher ratings to older workers but only does so for individuals who return to work at less than pre-injury earnings.

We evaluate the effectiveness of the age adjustment using a methodology similar to that employed in Chapter Five. Specifically, we take our sample of matched DEU and EDD data and compare the earnings losses to disability ratings for the individuals in our sample that receive age and occupation adjustments. We would expect that if the age adjustment operates appropriately, then workers observed with a positive or negative modifier would be observed with higher or lower earnings losses, respectively. The California schedule also provides adjustments for occupation. Our data do not provide a means to evaluate the post-1997 occupation data; however, a discussion of the occupation modifier is in Appendix C.

In this chapter, we consider one additional factor that is not considered in disability ratings in California but is in some other states: whether or not an individual returns to work. As we will demonstrate, return to work is an important predictor of the long-term economic consequences of a disability. Despite this, injured workers receive the same compensation whether or not they return to work. We argue that a *two-tier benefit system,* which provides relatively lower benefits to workers that receive an employment offer from the at-injury employer and higher benefits to those that do not, could improve the equity of disability benefits while also improving outcomes for disabled workers.

Age Adjustments

In California, all permanently disabled workers receive a modifier on their disability rating based on their age at the time of injury. The baseline age in the California system is 39, and individuals receive higher or lower ratings if they are above or below this age, respectively.

Consider an individual with a permanent disability assigned a standard rating of 15 percent who was 39 at the date of injury. Another individual with the exact same injury (and same standard rating) who was 25 at the date of injury would have the rating reduced to 12.25 percent, while someone who was 45 at the date of injury would have the rating raised to 16 percent. The rating for someone 21 or younger would be lowered to 11.5 percent, while the rating for someone 64 or older would be raised to 20 percent. The California disability rating system specifies the exact adjustment for each standard rating for each age between 21 and 64 at the time of injury.

Presumably, the assumption behind the higher ratings given to older individuals is that older people find it more difficult to adapt to permanent disabilities than younger people with equal levels of functional impairment. Thus, even though the physical restriction resulting from the disability is the same, the older worker will find it more difficult to work with the disability and hence will have a greater loss of ability to compete in the labor market. It is this theory that we examine in this section. If older workers have a greater loss of ability to compete for employment, given any standard disability rating, then we should observe higher earnings losses for those workers.

We test the effectiveness of the age modifiers using, in principle, the same methodology as the one described in Chapter Five. We use data on claims with summary ratings for which we have information on date of birth and three-year earnings losses. These observations are broken out into four age groups: 18 to 29, 30 to 39, 40 to 49, and 50 to 65. This left us with 80,667 observations.

Unfortunately, we cannot simply calculate the earnings losses for each group and report them as we did in the previous chapter. The reason is that we do not believe that the modifiers for age are unbiased. While we have data on the date of birth for injured workers, we have no such data on the date of birth for the comparison (control) workers. Selecting observations for analysis based on the date of birth of the injured worker can bias estimates of earnings losses, because the uninjured control workers could be any age. It essentially leaves us comparing the earnings of individuals from a fixed age group (the injured workers) with the earnings of individuals from a random age group (the control workers), making it impossible to distinguish whether the differences are because of differences in disability severity or differences in age.

Consider the case of an older worker. It is well established that older workers are more likely to exit the labor force at any given point in time than younger workers and, hence, probably have lower average earnings (or at least lower growth in earnings). Thus, if we select an older worker but leave the age distribution of comparison workers random, we are more likely to find younger workers in the comparison group. This can have the effect of overestimating the size of earnings losses, because the comparison workers are now relatively less likely to exit the labor force and more likely to experience an increase in earnings for a given disability status.[1]

If selecting observations for analysis based on the age of an injured worker produces (potentially) incorrect estimates of earnings loss, it would clearly make it difficult to evaluate the effectiveness of the age adjustments. If we are to estimate whether or not older workers suffer higher earnings losses, we need an estimate of earnings losses that is unbiased for different age groups. To obtain this estimate, we make the following assumption: The bias in earnings losses due to selecting observations for analysis based on the age of injured workers is constant across disability ratings. Given this assumption, the extent to which earnings losses are overestimated for older workers is the same for older workers with low disability ratings and for older workers with high disability ratings. Essentially, this assumption requires that the age distribution for comparison workers that is conditional on the age of the injured worker is independent of the disability rating.[2] Taken with the assumption that differences in earnings losses by older and younger workers in very-low-rated cases are due entirely to this age bias (and not to systematic differences in impairment), we can compute a set of "adjusted" earnings loss estimates that should reflect the correct age distribution.

In Table 6.1, we illustrate the expected bias due to selecting observations for analysis based on age that we use to adjust the earnings-loss estimates. Here, we focus on the 20,144 observations in our sample with a standard disability rating from 1 percent to 5 percent. The low-rated claims are useful for our purposes because we know from Chapter Five that the earnings losses for these cases are close to zero on average, and they are relatively insensitive to the disability rating, suggesting that variation in losses among age groups can be more easily attributed to the age bias (and not to differences in impairment). We see from Table 6.1 that the average proportional earnings loss across all age groups is 3.3 percent. We also see slightly higher earnings losses for younger workers, at 3.6 percent, and much higher losses

---

[1] The comparison workers are selected based in part on similar tenure at the at-injury employer. This selection criterion might lessen the possibility that younger and older workers are matched together but likely will not eliminate it completely.

[2] For example, let A represent the mean age of the comparison workers, I represent the age of the injured worker, and R the injured worker's disability rating. Formally, we can state our assumption as $E[A \mid I,R] = E[A \mid I]$.

Table 6.1
Estimating the Age Bias in Proportional Earnings Losses

Age Group	N	Proportional Losses: Standard Disability Rating of 1–5 Percent	Predicted Bias
All Ages	20,144	0.033 (0.003)	
18 to 29	3,790	0.036 (0.007)	0.003
30 to 39	6,495	0.021 (0.005)	−0.011
40 to 49	6,121	0.004 (0.004)	−0.028
50 to 65	3,738	0.096 (0.007)	0.064

NOTE: Standard errors are shown in parentheses. N = number of observations.

for the older workers, at 9.6 percent. The earnings losses for the two middle groups are lower than the average losses, likely reflecting the fact that workers between the age of 30 and 49 have more stable earnings profiles and are much less likely to exit the labor market.

We calculate the predicted bias by subtracting the average earnings losses across all groups from the average losses within each group. We then subtract this estimated bias for each age group from the estimated proportional losses for groups with higher ratings. The key point to remember is that this process will provide us with unbiased estimates of proportional losses *under the assumption that the age bias is constant across disability ratings*. If the age distribution of the comparison workers for some reason is different for workers with higher disability ratings, then our adjustment may not eliminate the age bias in earnings losses (it is possible that it could exacerbate it). While we believe this assumption is reasonable, it is not testable given our data, and so we cannot say for sure that it holds.

In Figure 6.1, we present the bias-corrected three-year proportional earnings losses for each of our four age groups by disability rating. Note that the earnings losses for the 1–5 percent disability rating group are identical for all age groups, because the bias corrections are calculated using this rating group. What is immediately evident from the table is that, after correcting for the age bias, there is no evidence that older workers experience higher long-term earnings losses. In fact, the youngest workers in our sample, the 18- to 29-year-olds, experience the highest proportional losses in all ratings groups. The two middle groups have relatively small proportional losses on average.

While the table certainly does not suggest that the earnings losses for different-aged workers are identical, it suggests that the differences are not necessarily large.

Figure 6.1
Corrected Three-Year Earnings Losses by Age and Disability Rating Groups

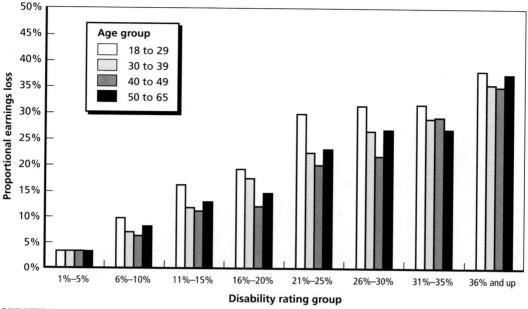

RAND MG258-6.1

Perhaps more important, it suggests that there is no linear relationship between earnings losses and age. It appears that disabled workers age 50 to 65 sometimes have higher losses and sometimes have lower losses than disabled workers age 30 to 39. Workers age 40 to 49 seem to have the lowest losses on average, while workers age 18 to 29 have the highest.

These results cast doubt on the effectiveness of the age modifiers used in the California system, at least with regard to targeting benefits toward the most disabled workers. The oldest workers do not appear to experience the highest earnings losses on average. In particular, there is little justification for the negative adjustments that apply to workers under 39 years of age. If anything, the results suggest that these workers should receive some kind of positive adjustment (at least those below 29 years of age). This is particularly true when we take into account that large, persistent *proportional* losses for young workers will result in substantially larger *cumulative* losses over the course of their working lives.

It is worth noting that while our bias correction was necessary to generate unbiased estimates of earnings losses (conditional on our assumption), if we had made no correction, our results would not have substantially changed. If we made no correction for the age bias, then our estimates would simply suggest that the earnings losses are much higher for workers below age 30 and above age 49 than they are for those in the middle. This would still argue against the current age modifiers. The finding that relies most heavily on our bias correction is that the oldest workers, the 50- to 65-year-olds, are relatively overcompensated given their earnings losses.

Return to Work

The common theme of most of RAND's studies on the adequacy of permanent partial disability benefits in California has been that injured workers suffer persistent earnings losses even five years after the date of injury. One of the driving forces behind these earnings losses is the fact that disabled workers in California are much less likely to work than their uninjured counterparts. Past RAND studies show that permanently disabled Californians are almost 20 percent less likely to be working five years after injury than their uninjured counterparts (Reville et al., 2001c).

It is not surprising that we observe disabled individuals being less likely to participate in the labor market. What is surprising, however, is how much more disabilities seem to limit work in California than in other states. Boden, Reville, and Biddle (2005) show that in comparison with New Mexico, Wisconsin, Oregon, and Washington, injured workers in California are much less likely to return to work subsequent to a permanently disabling injury than workers in those other states. In particular, workers in California are much less likely to return to the at-injury employer.

Return to the at-injury employer is important in this analysis because it is a strong predictor of the long-term economic outcomes of disabled workers. Figure 6.2 displays the estimated portion of accumulated three-year earnings losses due to disability for permanently disabled workers by their disability rating. The lighter gray bars in the figure show the average proportional losses for all disabled workers, regardless of whether they are observed returning to work. The darker gray bars represent the average three-year losses of workers who are observed at the at-injury employer four quarters (one year) after the date of injury. The black bars represent the average three-year losses for workers who are observed working eight quarters (two years) after the date of injury.

Figure 6.2 makes it clear that, at every level of severity, workers who return to the at-injury employer experience much lower long-term proportional losses than those who do not. While the differences among those groups with very low disability ratings (a rating between 1 and 10 percent) are very small, workers with medium or severe disabilities have much lower earnings losses if they return to the at-injury employer. For example, the overall proportional losses are approximately 12 percent for disabled workers with a disability rating between 11 and 20 percent, but the losses are just 8 percent for workers observed at the at-injury employer one year after injury and just 6 percent for those at the at-injury employer two years after injury. For more severe disabilities, such as those with ratings between 41 and 50 percent, the overall

Figure 6.2
Three-Year Proportional Earnings Losses for Injured Workers in California by Disability Rating Group and Return-to-Work Status

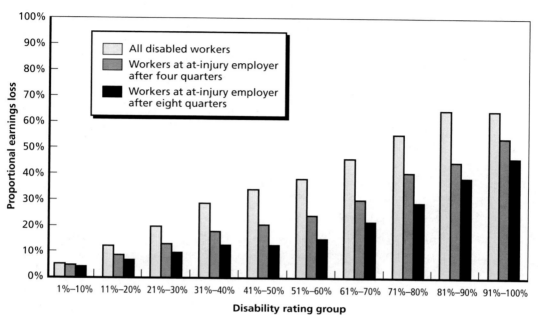

losses are approximately 34 percent compared with 20 percent for those working for the at-injury employer one year after injury and just 13 percent two years after injury.

Clearly, the return of workers to their at-injury employer is a strong predictor of lower long-term earnings losses. Note that Figures 6.1 and 6.2 do not indicate whether the worker is employed full time, so even modified work might have a positive impact on long-term earnings outcomes. When we consider these results along with the results of Boden, Reville, and Biddle (2005), which found that injured workers in California are much less likely to return to the at-injury employer than injured workers in other states, it is clear that poor return-to-work outcomes at least partly explain why long-term replacement rates are so low.

Adjusting Benefits to Reflect Return to Work

While California made no adjustment for disability benefits based on return to work prior to SB 899, other states have done so for many years. As discussed in Reville et al. (2001b), one means through which states make adjustments based on return to work is through the use of a two-tier benefit program. *Two-tier benefits* refer to the provision of lower PPD benefits to workers who exhibit greater earnings capacity, generally by receiving an offer of employment from the at-injury employer. The exact nature of the two-tier benefit varies in different states. In New Mexico, for instance, an injured worker with an "unscheduled" injury (also called a "whole body" injury, primarily to the head, neck, or back) is assigned a disability rating based on the degree of functional impairment. If the worker does not return to work, or returns to work at less than his or her pre-injury wage, a set of modifiers is applied to the rating, thereby offering bonuses for workers with lower predicted earnings capacity (specifically older workers, workers with less education or skills, and workers with lower physical capacity). Injured workers in Wisconsin become eligible for higher PPD benefits if their at-injury employers fail to rehire them at 85 percent or more of their pre-injury earnings. Oregon offers a sort of "three-tier" benefit program, in which benefits are higher if injured workers return to work at less than the pre-injury wage and higher still if they do not return to work at all. What all of these programs have in common is that they provide higher benefits to workers who are observed having worse labor-market outcomes.

The use of two-tiered benefit programs is not simply a means of improving equity; its primary intent is to improve return to work. A two-tier benefit can do this by providing employers with a greater incentive to rehire injured workers. Because an employer will have lower benefit payments if it brings back its injured workers, it has a greater incentive to accommodate the worker's disability and perhaps arrange for modified work. Figure 6.2 suggests that return to work could improve long-term outcomes, because return to the at-injury employer seems to correlate with much-lower proportional earnings losses over time. Of course, if California were to return more workers to the at-injury employer, we would not (necessarily) expect to observe the same difference in long-term outcomes as displayed in Figure 6.2. This is because the sample of workers who currently return to the at-injury employer might represent a *selected sample* of workers—those who are particularly adept at working with their disability or who work for employers that are particularly accommodating. Still, as long as the selection bias does not explain *all* of the observed differences in outcomes, then increasing return to the at-injury employer should improve earnings outcomes for injured workers.

Note that a two-tier benefit program provides unambiguous incentives to improve return to work only if the lower benefits are conditioned on the *offer* of work. If an injured worker had an offer to return to work with relatively low benefits but could receive higher benefits if he or she refused the offer, this situation could give the worker a perverse incentive to refuse the offer and take the higher benefits (and perhaps look for work from another employer). Making lower-benefit payments conditional on the offer of return to the at-injury employer, assuming that the workers have medical clearance to perform the work, provides employers with clear incentives to bring back to work the injured workers who can be productively employed without giving those workers any incentives to refuse the offer.[3]

While a two-tier benefit program should, in theory, promote return to work and potentially improve long-term employment outcomes, there is some question as to how such a program might impact the adequacy and equity of PPD benefits. Previous RAND studies have shown that, in general, injured workers in California experience significant uncompensated earnings losses (Peterson et al., 1997; Reville et al., 2001c). Would a two-tier system, which necessarily implies lower benefits for injured workers who return to work, worsen the adequacy of workers' compensation benefits in California?

Table 6.2 presents the proportional earnings losses and before-tax and after-tax replacement rates for injured workers in California by return-to-work status. The top part of the table illustrates the outcomes for workers three years subsequent to the date of injury, while the bottom part illustrates outcomes for workers five years subsequent to the date of injury. We separate the results by all injured workers and injured workers observed with earnings from the at-injury employer one year, two years, and three years after the date of injury. Having earnings from the same employer at which the disabling injury occurred over long time periods is a clear sign that the disability had less effect on an individual's career path, so we would expect those with longer tenure at the at-injury employer to have fewer earnings losses.

Table 6.2 clearly reinforces the results of Figure 6.2, in that workers who return to the at-injury employer for any significant length of time have much lower long-term proportional losses than those who do not.[4] The average proportional losses three years after the date of injury for all injured workers whether they return to work or not are 34.3 percent, but the losses fall almost by half to 17.2 percent for individuals observed working at the at-injury employer one year after the date of injury. We can also see from the table that the replacement rates are substantially higher for injured workers who return to the at-injury employer. While the before-tax replacement rates three years after injury are just 63.9 percent on average, they climb to 79.4 percent for workers observed working for the at-injury employer one year after injury and 98.5 percent for those working for the at-injury employer three years after injury. The replacement rates are lower for all groups five years after injury, as we can see with the replacement rate of just 53.1 percent before taxes for all workers. Still,

---

[3] Of course, it is also critical that the employment offer meet some minimum threshold of acceptability. If the lower tier of benefits were provided when the employer makes an offer that it knows would be unacceptable to the worker, because the job has drastically lower pay or worse working conditions, return to work would not be improved.

[4] Note that the workers who return to the at-injury employer are included in the "All Injured Workers" category, so we are underestimating the difference in outcomes between those that do and those that do not return to the at-injury employer.

Table 6.2
Proportional Losses and Replacement Rates for Disabled Workers in California by Return-to-Work Status, 1993 Injuries

	Proportional Earnings Losses	Before-Tax Replacement Rate	After-Tax Replacement Rate
Three Years After Injury			
All injured workers[a]	0.343	0.639	Not available
Returned to at-injury employer, year 1	0.172	0.794	1.049
Returned to at-injury employer, year 2	0.126	0.923	1.234
Returned to at-injury employer, year 3	0.109	0.985	1.325
Five Years After Injury			
All injured workers[a]	0.321	0.531	0.687
Returned to at-injury employer, year 1	0.176	0.587	0.777
Returned to at-injury employer, year 2	0.132	0.668	0.890
Returned to at-injury employer, year 3	0.108	0.717	0.960

[a] Includes only workers at insured firms in California.

we see that the replacement rates for those working for the at-injury employer at year 3 (71.7 percent) are almost 20 percentage points higher than the average replacement rate for all workers.

An important feature of workers' compensation benefits is that they are not taxable, implying that the "real" replacement rate is higher than the result of simply dividing benefits by wages. The far-right column of Table 6.2 simulates the after-tax replacement rates for workers.[5] One can see that the after-tax replacement rates are substantially higher for workers who return to the at-injury employer. While we do not have the three-year replacement rates for the entire sample, we can show that for the sample of workers who return to the at-injury employer the replacement rate is greater than 1.0. For those observed working for the at-injury employer three years after the injury, the after-tax replacement rate is 132.5 percent, meaning that the after-tax income of these workers was 32.5 percent higher than it was before the injury. Note that the five-year replacement rates are less than 1.0, although they are equivalent to 96 percent for those observed working for the at-injury employer three years after injury.

---

[5] For a discussion of the methods used to simulate the after-tax rates, see Peterson et al. (1997) and Reville et al. (2001c).

Promoting Return to Work in the New Reforms

Our results suggest that the adequacy of workers' compensation benefits as they are currently structured in California differs substantially according to whether or not an injured worker returns to work, particularly at the at-injury employer. Injured workers who continue working at the at-injury employer may actually receive benefits that exceed their earnings losses after tax considerations are taken into account, at least for some period of time after the date of injury.

The uneven replacement of lost earnings for workers with differing return to work outcomes was an area that was addressed in the recent reform bill SB 899. In fact, SB 899 amended Labor Code Section 4658 to read as follows:

(2) If, within 60 days of a disability becoming permanent and stationary, an employer does not offer the injured employee regular work, modified work, or alternative work, in the form and manner prescribed by the administrative director, for a period of at least 12 months, each disability payment remaining to be paid to the injured employee from the date of the end of the 60-day period shall be paid in accordance with paragraph (1) and increased by 15 percent. This paragraph shall not apply to an employer that employs fewer than 50 employees.

(3) (A) If, within 60 days of a disability becoming permanent and stationary, an employer offers the injured employee regular work, modified work, or alternative work, in the form and manner prescribed by the administrative director, for a period of at least 12 months, and regardless of whether the injured employee accepts or rejects the offer, each disability payment remaining to be paid to the injured employee from the date the offer was made shall be paid in accordance with paragraph (1) and decreased by 15 percent.

(B) If the regular work, modified work, or alternative work is terminated by the employer before the end of the period for which disability payments are due the injured employee, the amount of each of the remaining disability payments shall be paid in accordance with paragraph (1) and increased by 15 percent. An employee who voluntarily terminates employment shall not be eligible for payment under this subparagraph. This paragraph shall not apply to an employer that employs fewer than 50 employees.

Thus, under the new law, if the at-injury employer offers a permanently disabled worker appropriate (as defined by the administrative director) work for at least 12 months within 60 days of the injury being declared permanent and stationary, the disability benefits will be 15 percent lower than the prescribed levels. On the other hand, if the employer fails to make such an offer, then the disability benefits will be 15 percent higher than the specified level, leaving a 30 percent difference between an offer of return to work and no offer. Clearly, this policy can provide substantial incentives to employers to accommodate return to work.

It is impossible to say for sure what the impact of a two-tier benefit program would be in California. It should provide incentives to increase the frequency with which injured workers return to the at-injury employer, but how much impact a two-tier benefit system would have in practice is unknown. Likewise, results from past RAND studies suggest that a two-tier benefit could reduce long-term earnings losses for disabled workers, but how much so is also unknown. Our results suggest that offering lower benefits to workers who return to work could make PPD benefits more equitable, in the sense that it would reduce replacement rates for workers who return to the at-injury employer and increase them for those who do not. Ultimately, the impact of the two-tier benefit on return to work and the equity of benefits would depend largely on how the system is implemented.

CHAPTER SEVEN

Evaluating the Consistency of Disability Ratings in California

The previous chapter focused on how accurately California's permanent disability rating schedule targets higher benefits to more severely injured workers, both within and between impairment categories. In this chapter, we consider a different measure of the effectiveness of the rating schedule: the consistency with which medical information is incorporated into the disability rating process to produce the actual ratings. We define a *consistent rating schedule* to be one in which identical impairments of equal severity receive the same ratings. While it is naïve to suppose that any rating system will be perfectly consistent, a good system should minimize the variance in ratings assigned to similar impairments.

Any failure by the rating schedule, or the system for implementing it, to consistently provide similar ratings to similar impairments will be suggestive of inequity in California's permanent disability system. Additionally, inconsistency can impact the efficiency of the system by encouraging disputes. One important purpose of disability ratings is to provide information that allows benefit amounts to be determined with minimal dispute over the determination of impairment severity. However, if ratings vary substantially, injured workers who feel that they are not being sufficiently compensated may be encouraged to challenge the assigned rating. Employers, or the insurance companies liable for the permanent disability benefits of the employers' injured workers, likewise may have incentives to challenge disability ratings that they feel are too high. While litigation over some issues is a reasonable way to resolve disputes, litigation over disability ratings (which are intended to produce information that can reduce disputes) is costly and inefficient and potentially worsens the employment outcomes for disabled workers by placing them in an adversarial position with their employers.

In this chapter, we examine a key source of inconsistency in ratings: evaluations of the same injury by different physicians. Inconsistency arises in such cases because two physicians may have different opinions about the nature and severity of the same injury, particularly in a system that relies on subjective criteria. A second source of inconsistency is also a possibility in California. Because a rating specialist interprets the information provided by physicians and assigns the actual ratings, two raters looking at the same medical report might produce different ratings. While we were not able to completely distinguish between the two sources of inconsistency, the following discussion nevertheless provides some valuable information on the overall level of inconsistency in permanent disability ratings in California.

Data and Methods

To study the issue of inconsistency due to differences in physician evaluations, we take advantage of the fact that there are three kinds of ratings in the DEU data: applicant, defense, and summary. A *summary rating* is the most common type of rating, and it is the type of rating that we have focused on until now in this report. A summary rating is typically based on a report by a "qualified medical examiner," a randomly assigned physician who can plausibly be considered neutral to either party, or an "agreed medical evaluator," who is selected by both parties. An *applicant rating* is based on the medical report by a physician selected by the applicant (the injured worker), and a *defense rating* is based on the medical report by a physician selected by the defense (the payer—either the employer or the employer's insurer).

Table 7.1 illustrates the number of different types of ratings present in the DEU data.[1] While summary ratings are by far the most common (summary-only ratings account for more than half of our sample), in some cases there are applicant and defense ratings, or even all three ratings, for the same injury. While these cases represent a relatively small fraction of all types of ratings, the sample sizes are still large enough to allow us to study the extent to which physicians vary in their assessments of the same injury.

Table 7.1
Types of Disability Ratings in DEU Data, by Percentage and Number

Type of Rating for Individual Injuries	Percentage	Cumulative Percentage	Number
Applicant only	27.7	27.7	74,478
Defense only	8.5	36.2	22,838
Summary only	53.6	89.8	144,231
Applicant and defense only	6.1	95.9	16,328
Applicant and summary only	2.5	98.4	6,754
Defense and summary only	1.1	99.5	2,927
Applicant, defense, and summary	0.5	100.0	1,318
Total	100.0	—	268,874

[1] This sample is made up of all cases of each rating type in which both the disability category and final rating are present in the DEU database.

Our strategy involved identifying variation in physician evaluations by comparing differences in ratings for the same injury. Note, however, that because the different ratings we observe are often assigned by different raters, we cannot, in principle, distinguish variation in ratings due to physician differences from variation in ratings due to rater differences. However, if we think that certain physicians will provide a report that leads to a rating that is favorable to the party that selected the physician, whether intentionally or not, this gives us a method for inferring the extent to which ratings may differ.

Disability benefits increase as the disability ratings increase, so a report that is favorable to the applicant will lead to greater benefits, while a report favorable to the defense will lead to lesser benefits. Because the physicians that produce summary ratings can plausibly be considered to be neutral, their ratings should not lead to ratings that are systematically higher or lower than the *true rating* (the rating we would observe if we had a perfect, unbiased, error-free measure of severity).[2] By examining applicant, defense, and summary reports *for the same injury*, we can extract some information from the different rating types on the extent to which ratings in the California system differ due to variability in physician evaluations. Given that disability raters, like physicians who provide reports for summary ratings, can plausibly be considered to be neutral, any systematic differences among the ratings by physician type should be independent of rater inconsistency (in other words, the error by raters can be assumed to have a mean of zero).

This gives us the foundation for our methods in this chapter. If summary ratings should be approximately equal to the correct rating, at least on average, then we can check for any "biases" in ratings from other types of physician evaluations by comparing their ratings to the summary ratings. If physicians selected by the applicant tend to provide medical reports that are more favorable to the applicant, we would expect to have applicant ratings that are systematically higher than summary ratings. On the other hand, if the physicians selected by the defense tended to provide ratings that were more favorable to the defense, we would expect these ratings to be systematically lower than the summary ratings.

We make no assertion here about whether any such biases are the result of intentional action by physicians (collusion), or whether they are the result of each side having selected physicians with a known tendency to provide either higher or lower ratings (reputation). We simply test whether or not we find a very specific relationship; we expect applicant ratings to be higher than summary ratings, which should in turn be higher than defense ratings in the data. By observing how much higher and lower the applicant and defense ratings are, respectively, over the summary ratings,

---

[2] It is important to note that our assumptions about physicians (or raters, for that matter) may not hold for any particular individual. We simply argue that these relationships should hold *on average*.

we have a measure of the extent of upward and downward variation from the "true" rating in the California ratings system.

Our discussion here has focused on the expected difference between two ratings. While this parameter is certainly indicative of how much inconsistency there is in the California system, another important measure is the variance or spread of this difference. Unfortunately, our data do not allow us to decompose variance into variance attributable to physicians and variance attributable to raters. We will, however, be able to examine the total variance in rating differences that we observe.

Results

Differences in Ratings by Physician Type

To determine the extent of the disability rating differences by type of physician, we first examine the simple difference in average applicant and defense disability ratings. We estimate the difference using all 17,638 observations in our sample in which we observe both a final applicant rating and a final defense rating. Table 7.2 shows us that in these cases the average applicant disability rating is approximately 35.98 percent, while the average defense disability rating is 26.85 percent. Note that these ratings are high, which is most likely due to the fact that cases with higher severity involve more benefits and are therefore "higher stakes" cases, which in turn makes them more likely to wind up with the sort of disputes that lead us to observe multiple ratings.

Table 7.2 shows that the average difference between applicant and defense ratings in our sample is 9.12 rating percentage points. This difference represents an approximate 34 percent increase on the defense rating and is statistically significant at even the 1 percent level. This result strongly supports our assumption that ratings based on applicant-selected physician medical reports are higher than ratings based on defense-selected physician medical reports, by a significant margin. Moreover, the

Table 7.2
Average Difference in Ratings by Type of Physician, All Cases with Applicant and Defense Ratings

Applicant Rating	Defense Rating
35.98	26.85
(0.17)	(0.15)
Difference in ratings:	9.12 (+34%)
	(0.17)*

NOTE: Standard errors are shown in parentheses. * = Statistical significance at the 5 percent level.

magnitude of the difference between the applicant and defense ratings suggests that there is room for substantial inconsistency in the California system.

The use of summary ratings allows us to bound the upward and downward variation in ratings. With that in mind, we now examine the ratings differences in the 1,318 cases that have all three types of ratings for the same injury (see Table 7.3). Again, these cases tend to involve relatively severe impairments, with an average summary rating of 30.43 percent. The average applicant rating is 37.07 percent, a 6.63 percentage point increase over the summary rating (a difference of about 22 percent). The average defense rating is 28.29 percent, which is 2.15 percentage points, or 7 percent, lower than the summary rating. Both differences are statistically significant.

Once again, we find clear support for our initial hypothesis that the applicant rating is greater than the summary rating, which is in turn greater than the defense rating. Under the assumption that the error in the summary rating has a mean of zero, estimates of the upward variation in ratings is 6.63 rating points, and the downward variation in ratings is 2.15 rating points. The fact that the summary rating is closer to the defense rating on average, and by a fairly significant margin, suggests that there is more upward variation than downward variation in the California system.[3]

While the broad differences that we described are informative, the inconsistency in physician reports may differ over many dimensions. For example, whether justified or not, Southern California has the reputation of being more litigious than Central

Table 7.3
Average Difference in Ratings by Type of Physician, Cases with Applicant, Defense, and Summary Ratings

Applicant Rating	Summary Rating	Defense Rating
37.07	30.43	28.29
(0.65)	(0.65)	(0.58)
Difference in applicant and summary ratings:		6.63 (+22%)
		(0.64)*
Difference in defense and summary ratings:		−2.15 (−7%)
		(0.67)*

NOTE: Standard errors are shown in parentheses. * = Statistical significance at the 5 percent level.

---

[3] Some of this difference between upward and downward variation may be due to a scaling effect. In general, if the summary rating is bound between 0 and 100, and the average disability rating is 30 percent, we might expect that there is more room to increase ratings than to decrease them.

or Northern California, and this characteristic spills over to the workers' compensation system. If the frequency with which claims are disputed, or the effort and resources that are put into disputing claims, vary regionally, then we might expect to observe similar inconsistencies in physician medical reports.

We test the hypothesis that inconsistency is greater in Southern California by comparing the differences in applicant and defense ratings by region (see Table 7.4). Of the 17,638 cases with both applicant and defense reports, we were able to match 17,555 of the cases (more than 99 percent) to a region at the time of injury. A majority of the cases—11,202 or about 64 percent—occurred in the southern part of the state, while approximately 10 percent of the cases occurred in the Central Coast region, and about 26 percent occurred in Northern California.

Table 7.4 provides clear evidence that the inconsistency is considerably higher in Southern California. The average applicant rating in that part of the state is 38.72 percent, while the average defense rating is 26.84 percent, a difference of approximately 44 percent. The differences in the Central Coast and Northern regions are much smaller, although at 21 percent and 15 percent, respectively, they are still substantial.

In Table 7.5, we show the regional differences in ratings for the cases that have all three types of ratings. We were able to match 1,305 cases to regions: 743 in Southern California, 172 in the Central Coast, and 390 in Northern California. Once again, we find that the inconsistency is highest in the Southern region. In Southern California, the average summary rating for cases with all three types of reports is 31.86 percent, with the average applicant rating 7.92 points (25 percent) higher and the average defense rating 3.72 points (12 percent) lower. In the Central Coast region, the applicant rating is just 11 percent higher than the summary rating

Table 7.4
Difference in Ratings by California Region, All Cases with Applicant and Defense Ratings

	Applicant Rating	Defense Rating	Difference	N
Southern California	38.72	26.84	11.88 (+44%)	11,202
	(0.21)	(0.20)	(0.21)*	
Central Coast region	30.06	24.87	5.19 (+21%)	1,825
	(0.46)	(0.45)	(0.46)*	
Northern California	31.56	27.56	4.00 (+15%)	4,523
	(0.31)	(0.29)	(0.32)*	

NOTE: Standard errors are shown in parentheses. * = Statistical significance at the 5 percent level; N = number of observations.

Table 7.5
Difference in Ratings by California Region, Cases with Applicant, Defense, and Summary Ratings

	Summary Rating	Difference Between Applicant and Summary Rating	Difference Between Defense and Summary Rating	N
Southern California	31.86	7.92 (+25%)	–3.72 (–12%)	743
	(0.89)	(0.84)*	(0.85)*	
Central Coast region	29.35	3.18 (+11%)	–0.92 (–3%)	172
	(1.87)	(1.64)	(1.78)	
Northern California	28.44	5.62 (+20%)	0.33 (+1%)	390
	(1.10)	(1.21)*	–1.15	

NOTE: Standard errors are shown in parentheses. * = Statistical significance at the 5 percent level.

and the defense report is just 3 percent lower, with the latter difference being statistically indistinguishable from zero. The difference between applicant and defense ratings in Northern California is 20 percent, comparable to the difference in Southern California. However, the difference between the defense and summary ratings in Northern California is negligible.

These results suggest that there is substantial inconsistency in the California system. Moreover, the inconsistency appears to be far more pronounced in Southern California than in the Northern California or Central Coast regions. State region, however, is just one dimension by which we might expect the degree of differences to vary. Just as we supposed that the differences between the summary rating and the applicant and defense ratings might be larger in Southern California than in Northern California, we might also expect that the differences (and hence the inconsistency) also should be larger for "subjective" injuries, those that rely more on subjective than objective criteria for evaluation. The term *subjective* is sometimes used to describe the permanent disability rating system as a whole, but it is generally asserted that soft-tissue impairments, such as chronic back pain and carpal tunnel syndrome, and psychiatric impairments rely most heavily on the use of subjective evaluation criteria and therefore should have the greatest inconsistency in their ratings.

We can examine the differences in ratings by impairment type in Table 7.6 using the sample of all applicant and defense cases. For the purposes of this examination, we restrict the sample to those impairment types for which there are 100 or more observations for single-impairment cases and 80 or more observations for multiple-impairment cases. The top part of the table provides information for the single-impairment cases and the bottom part provides information for the multiple-impairment cases (for multiple impairments, there were not enough observations

Table 7.6
Difference in Ratings by Impairment Type, All Cases with Applicant and Defense Ratings

Impairment Type Claimed by Applicant	Defense Rating	Difference in Rating Points Between Average Applicant Rating and Average Defense Rating	Percentage Difference Between Average Applicant Rating and Average Defense Rating
Single-impairment cases			
General lower extremity	29.40 (1.53)	6.87*	23%
Knee	24.32 (0.50)	4.88*	20%
Ankle	23.16 (0.92)	5.64*	24%
Impaired hearing	18.24 (1.70)	−4.87*	−27%
Impaired finger: Four digits	17.84 (1.64)	5.03*	28%
Impaired finger: Five digits	19.86 (0.90)	4.68*	24%
Loss of grasping power	21.22 (0.44)	1.68*	8%
General upper extremity	24.44 (0.45)	6.84*	28%
Shoulder	17.31 (0.53)	0.86	5%
Elbow	20.04 (1.00)	1.15	6%
Wrist	23.92 (0.66)	3.53*	15%
Back	26.15 (0.33)	6.12*	23%
Psychiatric	32.46 (1.13)	3.63*	11%
Multiple-impairment cases			
Loss of grasping power and back	25.98 (0.97)	14.84*	57%
General upper extremity and back	30.04 (0.81)	16.68*	56%
Shoulder and back	28.51 (0.85)	11.41*	40%
Wrist and back	26.89 (1.48)	15.95*	59%
General lower extremity and back	26.20 (2.21)	22.64*	86%
Knee and back	32.20 (0.95)	13.13*	41%
Ankle and back	27.78 (2.46)	14.47*	52%
Psychiatric and back	32.52 (2.32)	30.57*	94%
Post-traumatic head syndrome and back	24.61 (2.02)	12.25*	50%

NOTE: * = statistical significance at the 5 percent level. Standard errors are shown in parentheses.

with combinations of three or more impairments to be included in the table). Applicant and defense medical reports can produce different ratings along two dimensions: the severity of the impairment or the nature (or type) of impairment. Thus, it can be difficult to classify the type of impairment for cases in which applicant and defense ratings differ. For Table 7.6, we classify cases as being of the type of impairment specified in the medical report by the physician selected by the applicant.[4]

---

[4] Thus, if the applicant-selected physician calls the impairment a "back impairment," then it falls under the "back" category, regardless of how it was labeled by the defense-selected physician. We use the applicant description solely for purposes of presenting the results, not because we think the assessments of applicant-selected phy-

The second column in Table 7.6 lists the average disability rating given by defense-selected physicians that is associated with each impairment type (the standard error appears in parentheses). The third column lists the increase (or decrease) in rating points in the defense rating associated with the applicant rating—i.e., it shows the difference equal to the applicant rating minus the defense rating. The fourth column shows the percentage increase (or decrease) over the defense rating.

The table shows that the applicant rating is larger than the defense rating for most injuries, often by more than 20 percent for the single-impairment cases. The differences in ratings are even more pronounced for the multiple-impairment cases, with the applicant rating more than 50 percent higher than the defense rating on average. The largest differences are found in the cases in which the applicant claims both psychiatric and back impairments, with the applicant rating 94 percent higher than the defense rating on average. The largest difference for the single-impairment cases is 28 percent, shared by both the "Impaired finger: four digits" and "General upper extremity" impairment categories. The smallest difference for the multiple impairment cases is 40 percent (for the shoulder and back impairments), while the smallest difference for the single-impairment cases is –27 percent (for hearing impairments.)[5]

What can we say about the general perception that more subjective ratings have higher inconsistency? In general, it is difficult to provide a definitive answer to this question, because there is no precise definition of subjectivity on which one can rely. Even impairments measured using objective criteria typically leave some room for subjectivity in assessment by physicians. The evaluation of back impairment in California is generally considered to be highly subjective, and the percentage difference between the average applicant rating and the average defense rating is relatively large—23 percent. Psychiatric impairments are also considered to be highly subjective, but the percentage difference between applicant and defense ratings for psychiatric impairments is relatively low (11 percent). Upper-extremity injuries may provide us with the best example for studying this issue. Shoulder and elbow impairments are generally considered to be more "objective" than wrist impairments because the ratings for those impairments are based more heavily on "objective" criteria, such as range of motion tests (see Reville et al., 2002a). Table 7.6 shows that the difference between applicant and defense ratings are statistically insignificant for the shoulder and elbow impairments, while for wrist impairments there is a statistically significant difference of 15 percent.

---

sicians are necessarily any more or less accurate. We find analogous results if we classify impairments based on the impairment description in the defense-selected physician medical reports.

[5] The smallest magnitude of positive differences is 5 percent for shoulder injuries, but because we expect applicant ratings to be higher than defense ratings, the smallest overall difference is for the hearing impairments (where defense ratings are actually higher).

While these results suggest that there may be greater inconsistency among the disability ratings for impairments that rely on more-subjective evaluation criteria, the results are far from conclusive. In general, it is difficult to interpret the results from Table 7.6 because of the aforementioned problem that the applicant-selected and defense-selected physicians might classify the type of impairment differently. The likelihood of the physicians classifying an injury differently could vary by the type of injury. For instance, it might be quite easy to classify a hearing impairment, but the precise nature of an upper-extremity impairment is often much harder to pin down. Therefore, a defense-selected physician may call something a shoulder impairment while an applicant-selected physician may call it a back impairment (or vice versa). Or, one physician may claim there is only a single impairment involved in the case, while the other might claim there are two or more impairments.

For instance, in the cases in our sample in which the applicant-selected physician provides a report that leads to a case being rated as a single impairment to the back, the defense submits a report that also leads to the case being rated as a single impairment to the back 93 percent of the time (for the cases with both applicant and defense ratings). However, for cases in which the applicant-selected physician provides a report that leads to a case being rated as a loss of grasping power, however, the defense-selected physician provides a report that leads to the case being rated as a single loss of grasping power impairment in just 39 percent of cases.[6] This classification will affect the difference between the applicant and the defense ratings, because injuries to different parts of the body are associated with different standard ratings.

Whether the difference between applicant and defense ratings was driven by physician reports of impairment severity or by the type of impairment would not matter, if we could be certain that both factors were actually chosen by the physician. However, because ultimately it is the disability raters who assign the impairment codes that signify the type of impairment in our data, we cannot be certain how often the differences in impairment types are due to different physician evaluations or to different rater interpretations of the evaluations. This makes it more difficult to interpret the observed differences in applicant and defense ratings across the different types of impairments displayed in Table 7.6 as an actual measure of differences in physician evaluations.

One solution to this problem would be to use the impairment type from the rating based on the summary-physician evaluations and compare the differences in applicant and defense ratings. We do not follow this strategy here because the sample sizes are quite small for all but a few impairment types. Instead, we focus on the subset of our sample of observations in which the applicant and defense ratings list the same type of impairment (i.e., both the number of impairments and type of impair-

---

[6] A more detailed table with information on cases in which the applicant and defense physicians agree on impairment types is provided in Appendix D.

ment). The differences between applicant and defense ratings by impairment type for these cases are shown in Table 7.7 (for some impairment types—e.g., Impaired finger: Four digits—shown in Table 7.6, there were not enough observations in which the applicant and defense reports agree to be included in Table 7.7).

For every single-impairment type except one shown in Table 7.7, the average percentage difference is higher than that in Table 7.6, while for the three multiple-impairment groups shown in Table 7.7, the difference is lower. This finding suggests that at least some of the differences in types of impairments are due to physicians describing impairments in ways that lead to more favorable ratings and are not just the result of differences in interpretation by raters. The difference between applicant and defense ratings for the three types of multiple impairments listed in Table 7.7 is close to 23 percent on average, while the average difference for the single-impairment types is about 27 percent. The effect of limiting the sample to cases in which the applicant and defense ratings agree on the type of more subjective impairments is less clear. The average percentage difference between applicant and defense ratings for back impairments rises to 31 percent, while the percentage difference between ratings for

Table 7.7
Difference in Ratings by Impairment Type, Cases with Applicant and Defense Ratings That Agree on Nature of Impairment

Impairment Type	Defense Rating	Difference in Rating Points Between Average Applicant Rating and Average Defense Rating	Percentage Difference Between Average Applicant Rating and Average Defense Rating
Single-Impairment Cases			
General lower extremity	28.79 (1.76)	7.75*	27%
Knee	23.05 (0.51)	6.41*	28%
Ankle	22.35 (1.00)	7.31*	33%
Impaired hearing	13.88 (1.28)	0.40	3%
Impaired finger: Five digits	21.61 (1.56)	5.59*	26%
Loss of grasping power	19.54 (0.64)	3.77*	19%
General upper extremity	25.57 (0.53)	6.23*	24%
Shoulder	13.24 (0.43)	4.58*	35%
Elbow	15.87 (1.10)	5.31*	33%
Wrist	23.65 (0.80)	4.58*	19%
Back	25.06 (0.35)	7.72*	31%
Psychiatric	29.37 (1.56)	12.01*	41%
Multiple-Impairment Cases			
General upper extremity and back	40.99 (1.39)	7.54*	18%
Shoulder and back	32.63 (1.26)	7.35*	23%
Knee and back	36.82 (1.29)	9.89*	27%

NOTE: * = statistical significance at the 5 percent level. Standard errors are shown in parentheses.

psychiatric impairments is even higher—41 percent, the largest difference in both percentage and levels. However, shoulder, elbow, and wrist impairments all have very similar, and statistically significant, differences.

In general, our results show that ratings for the same injury based on medical reports from different physicians vary substantially. Moreover, the difference is systematic in that ratings based on applicant-physician reports are higher than those based on defense-physician reports. The differences are more pronounced in Southern California, which suggests that the differences may be partly due to the litigiousness of the workers' compensation system. The fact that we find significant rating differences between applicant and defense ratings, even for what one would regard as an "objective" injury, may support this view.

Variance in Physician Differences

While the average differences in disability ratings based on applicant and defense reports are informative, they are not the only measure of inconsistency in the California system, as mentioned above. Another important measure of inconsistency is the variance, or spread, in ratings differences. For instance, stating that the applicant rating is higher than the defense rating on average is far different from saying that the applicant rating is always higher than the defense rating. Focusing on the variance in ratings will give us some idea of how often an applicant or defense rating "pays off," in the sense that it provides a more favorable rating than the "true" rating.

Table 7.8 provides information on the variance in the differences between applicant and defense ratings by region for all cases with applicant and defense ratings. The top row gives the variance numbers for all of California. The second column shows that the 75th percentile difference is 21.5, meaning that in 75 percent of the cases, the applicant rating is at least 21.5 rating points higher than the defense rating, a difference of 80 percent. The fourth column shows that the 25th percentile difference is –3.00, suggesting that in 25 percent of cases, the applicant rating is three or

Table 7.8
Variance in the Difference Between Applicant and Defense Ratings, Cases with Applicant and Defense Ratings

	75th Percentile Difference	Average Difference	25th Percentile Difference	IQR
All of California	21.50 (+80%)	9.12	–3.00 (–11%)	24.50
Southern California	25.00	11.88	0.00	25.00
Central Coast region	16.00	5.19	–5.00	21.00
Northern California	14.75	4.00	–6.84	21.59

NOTE: IQR = the *inter-quartile range* of the ratings difference, defined as the difference between the 75th percentile rating and the 25th percentile rating.

more points (or 11 percent) lower than the defense rating. These results suggest wide disparity in the reliability of the applicant rating to come in higher than the defense rating for different cases, suggesting that selecting your own physician fails to "pay off" more than a quarter of the time.

Table 7.8 also shows that the 75th and 25th percentile differences are both higher in Southern California than in the other two regions of the state. In Southern California, the 25th percentile rating is exactly zero, while for the Northern California and Central Coast regions it is –6.84 and –5, respectively. This finding suggests that the applicant-physician's medical report not only pays off more in the southern part of the state, it also pays off more frequently. Interestingly, when we look at the final IQR, which reports the inter-quartile range (the difference between the 75th and 25th percentiles), we see that it is fairly similar for all three regions. It is slightly higher in Southern California, but this is not surprising because we know from the results shown in Tables 7.4 and 7.5 that the average rating is also higher. This suggests that the spread of the distributions of ratings does not differ substantially in different parts of the state; rather, the ratings mean is simply higher in Southern California.

What does this analysis tell us about the inconsistency in the California system? First, it indicates that the rating process in California is highly variable. Getting a second rating on an impairment can be a risky proposition; even when a worker chooses his or her own physician to conduct a medical examination, the worker is likely to wind up with a worse rating at least a quarter of the time. Unfortunately, because we cannot separate the variance due to differences in physicians' medical reports from the variance due to different raters rating the same impairment in different ways, we cannot distinguish how much of this variance is due to raters and how much is due to the subjective nature of the California rating schedule. Nevertheless, the high IQRs displayed in Table 7.8 suggest that there is considerable uncertainty for injured workers in California about the size of their disability ratings and, therefore, the amount of compensation they will receive for permanent disabilities.

Consequences for Injured Workers

Until now, our attention has been focused on the inconsistency in ratings without explicitly considering the implications for the benefits received by injured workers. Specifically, how much better off are injured workers if they receive the applicant rating as opposed to the summary or defense rating? To answer these questions, we simulate the amount of benefits workers would receive under each rating type, assuming that the benefit increases under California Assembly Bill 749 (signed into law on February 15, 2002) are fully phased in by 2006 as intended. We assume that workers earn enough to receive the maximum weekly benefit of $230 if their disability rating is less than 70 percent and $270 if their rating is 70 percent or higher.

Table 7.9 lists the differences in estimated indemnity benefits for injured workers by physician type for all of California and the three regions in the state. In this discussion, we focus on the subset of cases with applicant, defense, and summary ratings and examine how the number of weeks the injured worker receives benefits and the total dollar amount of the indemnity benefits change with either the applicant or defense rating. The table shows that an injured worker receives benefits totaling about $37,249 for 154 weeks on average with the summary rating. If, instead, the injured worker receives the applicant rating, he or she will receive benefits for an additional 41 weeks on average, which amounts to an increase in average benefits of $9,967. On the other hand, if a worker receives the defense rating, the number of benefit weeks falls by 15.95, and the worker receives $4,326 less in benefits. The difference in benefits based on the summary rating and the applicant rating is more substantial, on average, than the difference in benefits based on the defense and summary ratings. This is not surprising, because we saw earlier that the average defense rating is closer to the average summary rating than is the average applicant rating. Still, it is clear that the selection of the physician on whose report the rating is based can have a significant impact on the benefits received by injured workers.

Table 7.9 also shows us that the differences in benefits are most pronounced in Southern California. In the southern part of the state, receiving the applicant rating as opposed to receiving the summary rating on average amounts to an increase of $12,022, or a more than 30 percent increase. Note that the percentage increase in benefits is higher than the percentage increase in the rating because of the nonlinear way in which ratings translate into benefits. If an injured worker receives the defense rating in Southern California, indemnity benefits then will be $6,687 lower on average, a decline of almost 17 percent. The differences in benefits from the applicant

Table 7.9
Injured Worker Indemnity Benefits by Physician Type and by Region, Cases with Applicant, Defense, and Summary Ratings

		Benefits Received with Summary Rating	Difference in Benefits (Applicant Rating Compared with Summary Rating)	Difference in Benefits (Defense Rating Compared with Summary Rating)
All of California	Weeks	154	41	−16
	Total indemnity	$37,249	$9,967	−$4,326
Southern California	Weeks	163	49	−25
	Total indemnity	$39,655	$12,022	−$6,687
Central Coast region	Weeks	149	17	−8
	Total indemnity	$36,443	$3,947	−$2,530
Northern California	Weeks	140	34	−1
	Total indemnity	$33,486	$8,482	−$642

rating versus the defense rating in the other two regions generally are smaller, although the $8,482 average increase from receiving the applicant rating in Northern California represents a substantial increase of more than 25 percent.[7]

A clear implication of this inconsistency is that there are significant gains for either side from litigation. If a party is able to dispute a claim and receive a rating based on his or her physician's medical report, then there is a substantial benefit in terms of higher or lower indemnity payments. In fact, it is possible that the total difference in potential awards might be understated. Evaluating physicians also estimate the need for future medical treatment, an important component of many awards. A physician's bias toward higher or lower ratings is likely to correlate with generous or conservative estimates of future medical needs, suggesting greater incentives for litigation than those implied by Table 7.9. While litigation over medical care or other aspects of a claim may represent the appropriate and necessary assertion of the rights of injured workers, litigation that is stimulated by inconsistency in disability ratings, which are intended to provide summarized medical information to reduce disputes, seems to be inefficient.

Table 7.9 also suggests that the incentives to litigate are strongest in Southern California. It is difficult to pinpoint the causality in this relationship, however. If, as is commonly asserted, litigation is more frequent in Southern California, it may be because the payout from selecting one's own physician is so high. On the other hand, it may be that in Southern California each side is better at physician shopping or physicians are simply more sympathetic to the parties that select them.

Summary of Key Findings

The analysis covered in this chapter focused on the extent of inconsistency in the California rating schedule. There are two potential sources of inconsistency: physician ratings and raters. In our study of inconsistency from physician ratings, we examined cases that included multiple ratings for the same injury. These multiple ratings are based on reports from physicians selected by applicants or payers or on reports by physicians not selected by either party, who can plausibly be considered neutral. Thus, we expect to find the ratings from applicant or defense physicians to systematically favor the applicant or defense side, respectively, and we expect the ratings from summary physicians to be unbiased. This assumption suggests that the differences we observe in our analysis do not represent the expected difference from two randomly selected physicians who evaluate the same injury. Rather, our analysis

---

[7] Note that the average benefits for the defense rating in Northern California being smaller than the average benefits for the summary rating, even though the average rating is slightly higher, is a function of the nonlinear nature of the benefit schedule.

produces a measure of the amount of discretion that is exerted by physicians (inadvertently or not) on behalf of either side.

As stated above, our results suggest that there is a significant amount of inconsistency in permanent disability ratings in California. Applicant ratings tend to be 22 percent higher than summary ratings on average, while defense ratings tend to be 7 percent lower than summary ratings on average. The inconsistency varies substantially among the three regions of the state, which is somewhat surprising given that they are using the same schedule. Nevertheless, applicant ratings in Southern California are 25 percent higher than summary ratings, while defense ratings are 12 percent lower than summary ratings. In Northern California, the applicant ratings are 20 percent higher than the summary ratings, but there is essentially no difference between the summary and defense ratings. The difference between applicant and defense physicians is unambiguously positive in the most prevalent impairment types.

We also find that the differences between applicant and defense ratings are highly variable, another indication of inconsistency in California's permanent disability ratings. The applicant rating is at least 11 percent lower than the defense rating for 25 percent of all cases in which we observe both types of ratings, while for another 25 percent of all such cases it is at least 80 percent higher. This result illustrates just how much uncertainty there is in permanent disability ratings in California. The differences we discuss have important consequences for injured workers (as well as for payers), because obtaining the applicant rating instead of the summary rating means an increase in indemnity benefits of more than $9,000 on average, while obtaining the defense rating means a decrease in indemnity benefits of more than $4,000.

Perhaps the most pressing policy question regarding inconsistency in ratings is how much of it is due to the California rating schedule. Unfortunately, our analysis cannot answer this question. Even though California has adopted a more objective system (based on the *AMA Guides* [American Medical Association, 2000]), substantial differences across ratings by different physicians still might remain.[8] In general, we expect that any workers' compensation permanent disability system that relies on advocacy to resolve claims will have some inconsistency in disability ratings.

---

[8] For example, Boden (1992) found large differences among *AMA Guide* ratings by different physicians for the same injuries in the state of Maryland. This suggests that the *AMA Guides* do not eliminate all subjectivity from the evaluation process.

CHAPTER EIGHT

Conclusions

This report provides an in-depth review of the California system for evaluating permanent partial disabilities. It offers substantial discussion of institutional challenges and solutions regarding the evaluation and compensation of permanent disabilities both in and out of California, and provides a number of additional empirical analyses to supplement the results provided in an earlier interim report (Reville et al., 2003). It evaluates the ability of the California permanent disability rating system to predict the lost earnings that disabled workers suffer, and the consistency with which those ratings are assigned. Additionally, the report provides a methodology for using empirical evidence to inform the process of evaluating permanent disabilities, which has implications that extend beyond California. Moreover, our evaluation in this report will serve as a useful benchmark for future examinations of the reforms instituted by SB 899. In this chapter, we summarize our findings and discuss them within the context of the recent and pending changes to the California disability rating system.

Key Results

One of the key questions we wanted to address with this study was whether or not the California permanent disability rating schedule targets benefits appropriately to workers. Our answer to this question appears to be a qualified yes. The California system appears to function reasonably well with respect to the *vertical* equity criterion (see Chapter Two for a definition of vertical and horizontal equity and Chapter Five for further discussion). On average, we can say that workers with more-severe impairments (in terms of greater lost earnings resulting from an injury) appear to receive higher ratings and, therefore, higher benefits. This appears to be true for workers within impairment types as well. However, the performance of the system on average masks some serious issues of fairness with regard to how different impairments are compensated. In other words, there appear to be serious *horizontal* equity problems. We found, in fact, substantial and systematic variation in proportional earnings losses for impairments to different regions of the body, even though these impairments have very similar ratings.

We also call into question the appropriateness of the California system's use of age as an adjustment factor. The California system operates under the assumption that permanent disabilities are more disabling for older workers, specifically those above age 39, and less disabling for younger workers. Our results suggest that the relationship between age and earnings losses is not so clear. In general, we do not find substantial evidence of large disparities between the earnings losses associated with similarly rated claims for injured workers of different ages (focusing on the ratings *before* adjustment for age). What evidence we do find suggests that, if anything, the youngest workers face the highest cumulative earnings losses from disability three years post-injury. This finding suggests that the age adjustment does little to enhance equity, and may even detract from it.

This report also demonstrates that a disabled individual's ability to return to work, particularly to return to work at the at-injury employer, is a strong predictor of long-term earnings losses. Specifically, individuals who are observed having returned to work for the at-injury employer even just four quarters after injury have significantly lower future earnings losses than individuals who do not return to work or who return to work at another employer. This finding suggests that introducing a program that makes benefits contingent on returning to work, without providing perverse work disincentives for returning to work, could improve the equity of disability benefits in California. We discuss some programs that have been introduced in other states, most notably a two-tier benefit system that gives lower benefits to injured workers who receive a legitimate offer of return to work by the at-injury employer (see Chapter Six).

Another question that we addressed in this study was whether or not there appears to be systematic inconsistency in ratings based on medical reports for the same injured worker by different physicians (i.e., physicians selected by the applicant or selected by the defense) and whether this inconsistency provides incentives for litigation. On average, we found that there are substantial differences in the ratings that are produced when the evaluations of different physicians are used. Physicians selected by applicants routinely provide higher ratings than physicians selected by the defense, and these differences can have a significant effect on the benefits received by injured workers. This finding suggests that there is inconsistency in ratings and that this inconsistency may encourage disputes. Interestingly, most of the inconsistency appears to be concentrated in Southern California.

The New California Rating System

This report was prepared during a period of radical change in the permanent disability rating system in California. As we have stated, SB 899 introduced sweeping reforms to the California system for compensating permanent partial disabilities. The rating system, in particular, was the target of many changes, and these changes will have a direct effect on the many aspects of the system examined in this study. Perhaps most notably, the disability ratings in California are no longer to be based on the 1997 rating schedule; instead, the injury descriptions and standard ratings are to be based on the *AMA Guides* (American Medical Association, 2000). However, these ratings are also to incorporate data of the sort used in this study and in Reville, Seabury, and Neuhauser (2003).

We expect that the adoption of the *AMA Guides* will increase the level of objectivity in the California system. Certainly, it will increase the system's reliance on objective medical evidence of disability. From our results, it is clear that physicians are often unable to agree on the type or even the number of impairments that an injured employee may have, to say nothing of the severity of the impairments. A more objective system could provide benefits in that it could both ensure that the appropriate level of benefits are assigned to injured workers and perhaps reduce the incentives to litigate. Reductions in the inconsistency in ratings by different physicians should lower the expected gains of disputing a claim. Thus, we would expect to see lower levels of costly litigation, something that would be beneficial to both workers and employers. Reductions in the inconsistency in ratings would also increase confidence that the system is performing fairly and efficiently.

It is important to note that moving to an objective basis for disability ratings, such as the *AMA Guides,* will not by itself eliminate inconsistency. Our results suggest that the extent of inconsistency varies considerably within the state, which in turn suggests that the old rating system alone was not enough to explain the wide differences between physicians' evaluations of a worker's injury. Perhaps the room for physicians to make differing evaluations is less under the *AMA Guides*, but this has not been demonstrated empirically. It is also worth noting that although subjectivity may have been eliminated from the system by adoption of the *AMA Guides* approach to describing impairments, some of it may be reintroduced by the new rules on apportionment introduced by Labor Code Sections 4663 and 4664. These new guidelines require physicians to make a determination of the fraction of permanent disability that is directly attributable to industrial factors for every new permanent disability case. However, there do not appear to be any clear scientific guidelines to aid physicians in determining the percentage of disability caused by industrial factors, opening a new avenue for physician inconsistency to enter the system. And, given that the new legislation essentially makes the apportionment of impairment to industrial and non-industrial factors (see Chapter Four) a multiplier on the permanent disability award, physicians differing widely enough on apportionment will provide an incentive for litigation.

We also expect that adoption of the *AMA Guides* approach to describing impairments will reduce the number of injured workers eligible for permanent disability benefits; in particular, workers with work restrictions resulting from chronic pain who do not have accompanying physical damage or pathology will no longer receive permanent disability benefits. This change will serve to lower employer costs directly and will also reduce the potential for abuse of the system. On the other hand, adoption of the *AMA Guides* approach will also lower benefits to some injured workers who have significant barriers to employment and reduce adequacy in a system that is already providing benefits that replace a lower fraction of lost earnings than many other states replace.

Another recent key reform is the aforementioned requirement that the impairment ratings based on the *AMA Guides* be adjusted to reflect differences in average earnings losses. This adjustment is intended to reduce the disparities in compensation for different types of injuries (we outline those disparities in Chapter Five). We show that, on average, a worker with an impaired shoulder, for example, now receives much lower benefits than a worker with a knee impairment of equal or even lesser severity (as measured by proportional earnings losses). Reordering the ratings to be consistent with average proportional losses for each impairment can promote equity in the system.

The recent reforms also require that the empirical data used to revise the disability ratings be updated after five years to reflect changes in earnings losses for injured workers during the intervening years. This requirement will provide a potential feedback loop from changes in employment patterns among injured workers that may result from changes in, for instance, employer practices after injury or changes in medical technology. The ratings revision will allow the system to remain equitable over time and will also allow improved return to work in the system, which could result in reductions in employer costs for permanent disability in the long run.

Finally, California introduced a two-tier benefit system to both improve the equity of compensation and encourage employers to rehire disabled workers. Under the new reforms, there will be a 30 percent difference in benefits between workers who do or do not receive an offer of return to work at the at-injury employers (15 percent lower benefits for workers who do receive an offer, 15 percent higher benefits for those who do not). This two-tier system makes for a more equitable PPD system, because workers with similar ratings who return to work tend to have lower earnings losses, for obvious reasons. The system encourages return to work because employers will be liable for lower benefit payments for disabled workers who receive an employment offer. If successfully implemented, such a program has the potential of both improving the equity of benefits and reducing the overall economic impact of disabling injuries on workers. This change, in combination with an additional program adopted with SB 899 that provides funding assistance to employers to pay for workplace modifications for disabled workers, holds out the possibility of a significant shift in the California workers' compensation system toward an improved rate of reemployment of permanently disabled workers. If these reforms significantly increase wages for injured workers, then they may improve outcomes for both workers and employers.

Future Research and Possibilities for Additional Reform

While SB 899 addressed a number of important issues regarding the rating of permanent disabilities in California, there remain unanswered questions about what the system will look like in the future. Not the least of these questions is, as we discuss in this section, how should the new reforms be implemented? Another question is whether or not the new rating schedule will outperform the old one in terms of the equity and adequacy of benefits. While the use of objective medical evidence made the *AMA Guides* a popular alternative to the California schedule, the *AMA Guides* are not uncontroversial and have problems of their own. Moreover, the *AMA Guides'* impairment ratings have not been empirically verified as measures of disability, so even with the adjustments *across* impairments (which have complications which we discuss later in this section), there is no guarantee that the new schedule will perform as well *within* impairments as the old system. Another important question is whether the reforms will do anything to reduce the number of disputes over PPD claims in California. The number of disputes has long been recognized as a serious problem in California. If the introduction of the *AMA Guides* improves the consistency of the system, it may also reduce disputes, as might provisions designed to improve the speed of delivery of medical care to injured workers. However, reforms such as apportionment to industrial causation and the two-tier benefit structure could also promote disputes, so the net effect of the new reforms bears watching.

Implementation is also a critical issue in going forward with the reforms. One of the key implementation challenges with the new disability rating schedule is that the earnings-loss estimates reported here and in the interim report, which are the data to be used to generate the adjustments in the new schedule, are based entirely on injury descriptions used by the old California rating schedule. The new legislation requires the rating adjustments to be applied to the ratings from the *AMA Guides,* but the injury descriptions in the two systems are very different. At the time of this writing, there is no crosswalk that can be used to link the earnings-loss estimates in our data to the *AMA Guides* injury descriptions. To see why this lack of a crosswalk presents an implementation challenge, consider the case of back injuries, which make up more than 30 percent of injuries in our data. The *AMA Guides* make distinctions among the cervical, thoracic, and lumbar areas of the back, whereas the California system uses a single classification for all three areas.

Implementation challenges aside, the rating schedule adopted under the new reforms will be more empirically based than any rating schedule before it. Still, there is potentially room to further incorporate empirical evidence on earnings losses. For

example, the pre–SB 899 approach to mapping disability ratings into weeks of benefits and maximum benefit amounts continues under the new system. Suppose, alternatively, that the rating for a particular injury exactly equals the predicted proportional earnings losses for a worker with that injury.[1] If a worker with an injury that
results in a particular loss of range of motion to the shoulder on average loses 10 percent of earnings over the years after the injury, that worker will receive a disability
rating of 10 percent. Under the SB 899 system, this 10 percent rating would result in
30 weeks of benefits at a given maximum weekly amount. An alternative approach
would, for example, pay $(2/3) \times (10\% \times$ pre-injury wage$) \times (520$ weeks$)$. If the pre-
injury wage used to calculate benefits included a cost-of-living adjustment, this approach would guarantee a two-thirds replacement rate for ten years after injury for a
worker who would have experienced stable real wages (the 2/3 rate is commonly re-
garded as being adequate).[2] The key advantages of this method are that it would be
straightforward to verify the adequacy of the system, and the transparency of the approach would hopefully improve confidence in the system. Furthermore, diminish-
ment of wage losses that result from improved return to work would ultimately
(through schedule revisions) lead directly to lower disability rating numbers; the adequacy of benefits would remain the same, and at the same time, the cost of the system to employers would be reduced. The system under SB 899 may have some of
these features, but without establishing the replacement rate automatically through a
formula for converting ratings into benefits, the system loses some transparency.

California's troubled workers' compensation permanent disability system has
faced, and continues to face, significant change. It seems likely that the changes will
result in lower costs to employers, which is desirable to the extent that these costs are
the result of inefficiencies in the system. However, it is important to consider the
impact of the reforms on the adequacy of permanent disability benefits, particularly
given the uncertainties about how the system will be implemented. A number of
studies by RAND have suggested that California's PPD benefits consistently fall
short of the benchmark adequacy standard of two-thirds wage replacement. Certain
elements of the new system, such as provisions that promote the return to work of
injured workers, may improve the adequacy of the system. On the other hand, the
reforms to the permanent disability rating system may lead to reductions in benefits
(depending on how the schedule is formulated) and may eliminate benefits entirely
for some claimants. Ultimately, the overall impact on the adequacy of benefits will

---

[1] It is not clear whether the average ratings will equal average proportional losses under the new system introduced by SB 899. SB 899 requires that the relative differences across impairments reflect differences in proportional wage losses, but the actual rating number may not equal the proportional wage losses associated with that
injury.

[2] Benefits would fall short of the two-thirds adequacy standard for workers who would have experienced real
wage growth. Trying to incorporate prospective estimates of real wage growth into a benefit schedule, however,
seems fraught with both conceptual and practical difficulties.

depend on the extent to which workers receive lower benefits compared with the extent to which return to work increases. The administrators of the California workers' compensation system should make it a priority to closely monitor these features of the system to ensure that both workers and employers benefit from the recent reforms.

Operational Approaches to Compensating Permanent Partial Disability

In this report, we have emphasized that PPD benefits are the most controversial and complex type of workers' compensation cash benefit. One reason for this complexity is that the operational procedures for PPD benefits vary widely among the states.[1] In Chapter Two, we argued that the primary (if not sole) reason for PPD benefits is to compensate for work disability—i.e., the loss of earning capacity or actual wage loss. Of significance to the discussion in this appendix is that among those states in which work disability is the sole reason why PPD benefits are paid, many use a different permanent consequence of injury or disease (see Figure 2.2) as a proxy or predictor of the extent of work disability. For example, many states operationally determine the amount of PPD benefits by measuring the seriousness of a worker's permanent impairment (PI), on the assumption that the PI rating will predict the extent of lost wages that will result from the impairment. This appendix supplements Chapter Two by providing an overview of the various operational approaches for PPD benefits that are found in U.S. and Canadian jurisdictions.

Three Operational Approaches for Determining Work Disability Benefits

Three basic operational approaches for determining work disability benefits, plus variants of each of those approaches, are shown in Table A.1.[2] The operational approaches represent the building blocks for PPD benefits systems. The differences among the three basic operational approaches depend on which of the permanent consequences shown in Figure 2.2 is used as a proxy for or direct measure of work disability.

---

[1] This appendix is based in part on Berkowitz and Burton (1987), Burton (1996), and Barth and Niss (1999).

[2] This three-category scheme is adapted from the taxonomy in Berkowitz and Burton (1987).

The Permanent Impairment Approach

The first basic operational approach, the *permanent impairment approach*, evaluates the seriousness of the worker"s permanent impairment and/or functional limitations resulting from the work-related injury or disease.[3] An impairment rating is made, which is then used to determine the amount of the worker's PPD benefits. While the only permanent consequences that are measured are the permanent impairment

Table A.1
Three Operational Approaches for Determining Permanent Disability Benefits

1. The Permanent Impairment Approach

1.A. The "Pure" Permanent Impairment Approach
  1. The worker is given a PI rating based on the extent of his or her permanent impairment/functional limitations, and
  2. The worker's PPD benefits are determined by multiplying the PI rating by a dollar amount per PI point that does not vary among individuals on the basis of their pre-injury wages.

1.B. The Permanent Impairment and Pre-Injury Wage Approach
  1. The worker is given a PI rating based on the extent of his or her permanent impairment/functional limitations, and
  2. The duration of the PPD benefit is determined by multiplying the PI rating by a duration specified in the statute or workers' compensation agency rule, and
  3. The weekly PPD benefit is determined by multiplying the worker's pre-injury wage by a percentage (e.g., 66-2/3 percent). The weekly benefit is subject to minimum and/or maximum weekly amounts.[a]

2. The Loss of Earning Capacity Approach

2.A. The "Ad Hoc" Loss of Earning Capacity Approach
  1. The worker is given an LEC rating based on the facts of the particular case, which include the worker's PI rating and other factors such as the worker's age, occupation, education, and prior work experience.
  2. The duration of the PPD benefit is determined by multiplying the LEC rating by a duration specified in the statute or workers' compensation agency rule, and
  3. The weekly PPD benefit is determined by multiplying the worker's pre-injury wage by a percentage (e.g., 66-2/3 percent). The weekly benefit is subject to minimum and/or maximum weekly amounts.[a]

2.B. The Loss of Earning Capacity by Formula Approach
  1. The worker is given an LEC rating based on a formula, which considers the worker's PI rating and other factors such as the worker's age, occupation, and education.
  2. The duration of the PPD benefit is determined by multiplying the LEC rating by a duration specified in the statute or workers' compensation agency rule, and
  3. The weekly PPD benefit is determined by multiplying the worker's pre-injury wage by a percentage (e.g., 66-2/3 percent). The weekly benefit is subject to minimum and/or maximum weekly amounts.[a]

2.C. The "Pure" Loss of Earning Capacity Approach
  1. The worker is given an LEC rating based on the facts of the case or based on a formula.
  2. The LEC rating is used to determine the amount of PPD benefits, using a formula that does not vary among workers on the basis of their pre-injury wages.

---

[3] The rating systems for this approach typically contain a mixture of impairment ratings (e.g., amputations are given a specified rating without any requirement to measure the resulting loss of function) and functional limitations ratings (e.g., loss of the use of a limb typically is rated by examining the loss of function caused by the injury).

Table A.1—Continued

---

3. The Actual Wage Loss Approach

3.A. The "Pure" Actual Wage Loss Approach

1. The worker's actual wage loss is (a) the worker's projected wages in the permanent disability period[b] minus (b) the worker's actual earnings in the permanent disability period.

2. The worker must demonstrate that the actual wage loss was due to the effects of the permanent impairment and was not because of other factors, such as the worker's voluntarily retiring or withdrawing from the labor force, or refusing a legitimate job offer, or general economic conditions, and

3. If the worker's actual wage loss is zero (or a negative number), there are no PPD benefits.

4. The duration of the PPD benefit depends on the duration of the worker's actual wage loss (subject to a statutory maximum on duration), and

5. The weekly PPD is determined by multiplying the actual wage loss by a percentage (e.g., 66-2/3 percent). The weekly benefit is subject to minimum and/or maximum weekly amounts.[a]

3.B. The Limited Actual Wage Loss Approach

1. The worker's actual wage loss is (a) the worker's projected wages in the permanent disability period[b] minus (b) the worker's actual earnings in the permanent disability period.

2. The worker must demonstrate that the actual wage loss was due to the effects of the permanent impairment and was not because of other factors, such as the worker's voluntarily retiring or withdrawing from the labor force, or refusing a legitimate job offer, or general economic conditions, and

3. The worker's maximum compensable wage loss is the workers' projected wages in the permanent disability period times either (c) the worker's LEC rating or (d) the worker's permanent PI rating; and/or the worker's maximum compensable wage loss is the actual wage loss in excess of a threshold that is a percentage of the worker's pre-injury wage.[c]

4. The worker's compensable wage loss is the lesser of the worker's actual wage loss or the worker's maximum compensable wage loss.

5. If the worker's compensable wage is zero (or a negative number), there are no PPD benefits.

6. The duration of the PPD benefit depends on the duration of the worker's compensable wage loss (subject to a statutory maximum on duration), and

7. The weekly PPD is determined by multiplying the compensable wage loss by a percentage (e.g., 66-2/3 percent). The weekly benefit is subject to minimum and/or maximum weekly amounts.[a]

---

[a] In a few jurisdictions, the duration of the PPD benefits is fixed and the PI rating is used to help determine the weekly PPD benefit.

[b] In most workers' compensation programs, the worker's projected wages in the permanent disability period are the same as the worker's pre-injury wages.

[c] The choice among the worker's loss of earning capacity rating or the worker's permanent impairment rating or the threshold linked to pre-injury wages varies among jurisdictions.

---

and/or functional limitations, these consequences are assumed to serve as a predictor or proxy for the actual wage loss (work disability) that will result from the permanent impairment or functional limitation.

The first variant of the PI approach is the *"pure" permanent impairment approach*. As indicated in Table A.1, the only worker-specific factor that affects the amount of PPD benefits in the "pure" permanent impairment approach is the size of the PI rating. The size of the PI rating presumably provides only a very rough proxy for the worker's actual loss of wages, but a few jurisdictions nonetheless rely on this approach for work disability benefits. The second variant of the PI approach is *the permanent impairment and pre-injury wage approach*. This approach involves multiplying the PI rating by a weekly benefit that is largely determined by the worker's weekly wage prior to the workplace injury.

The Loss of Earning Capacity Approach

The *loss of earning capacity approach* considers the seriousness of a worker's permanent impairment and functional limitations and other factors that may affect the loss of the worker's earning capacity resulting from an injury. These factors may include the worker's age, prior education, and prior work experience. In addition, factors such as the job opportunities in a given location may be considered. A particular jurisdiction may decide to incorporate any or all of these into the disability evaluation process and then use whichever factors it settles on to produce ratings of the injured worker's loss of earnings capacity. In turn, that rating is used to determine the duration (or, in some jurisdictions, the weekly amount) of the PPD benefits. Loss of earning capacity is presumably used as a proxy for the actual wage loss that is expected to result.

The first variant of the LEC approach is the *"ad hoc" loss of earning capacity approach*. The extent of the loss of earning capacity is decided based on the facts of the case, which may vary from case to case in the same jurisdiction depending on the purview of the parties (including the administrative law judge) involved in the case. This approach multiplies the LEC rating by a duration specified in the statute (such as 1,000 weeks) that represents the "whole person" to determine the duration of benefits for a partially disabled worker. The weekly benefit is calculated as a percentage of the worker's weekly wage prior to the workplace injury.

The second variant of the LEC approach is the *loss of earning capacity by formula approach*. The worker's PI rating is modified by a formula that considers factors, such as the worker's age or occupation, to determine the loss of earning capacity. This approach multiplies the LEC rating by a number of weeks for each percentage point of the rating to determine the duration of the PPD benefits for a partially disabled worker. The weekly benefit is calculated as a percentage of the worker's weekly wage prior to the workplace injury.

The third variant of the LEC approach is the *"pure" loss of earning capacity approach*. The worker's loss of earning capacity is determined based either on the facts of the particular case or on a formula. The LEC rating is then multiplied by a number of weeks for each percentage point of the rating to determine the duration of the PPD benefits. The weekly benefit is the same for all workers, and thus the benefit does not vary among workers on the basis of their pre-injury wages.

The Actual Wage Loss Approach

The *actual wage-loss approach* determines the actual wage loss due to a work-related injury by comparing the worker's earnings in the period after the date of MMI with the worker's earnings before the date of injury. The duration and amount of PPD benefits are then related to the duration and amount of actual wage loss.

The first variant of the AWL approach is the *"pure" actual wage loss approach*. As shown in Table A.1, this approach defines actual wage loss as the difference between the worker's projected earnings in the permanent disability period and the worker's actual earnings in that period. If the worker can demonstrate that the actual wage loss was due to a workplace injury or disease, the weekly PPD benefit is calculated as a percentage of the actual wage loss and is paid for the duration of the wage loss (subject to statutory limits on the duration).

The second variant of the AWL approach is *the limited actual wage loss approach*. The distinguishing feature of this approach is that the worker's compensable wage loss is limited by the extent of the worker's loss of earning capacity, or by the extent of the worker's permanent impairment, or by the amount of actual wage loss above a threshold that is a percentage of the worker's pre-injury wage, or by a combination of these factors. For example, if the worker's actual earnings in the permanent disability period are 75 percent below the projected earnings, but the worker is considered to have lost only 25 percent of his or her pre-injury earning capacity, then the PPD benefits will be based on the 25 percent figure. Another example is a worker with pre-injury wages of $500 per week and an actual wage loss of $100 per week in the permanent disability period, but the state limits compensable wage loss to the amount in excess of 15 percent of the worker's pre-injury wages; the compensable wage loss would then be only $25 per week.

Operational Approach for Nonwork Disability Benefits

As previously mentioned, a few jurisdictions, in addition to compensating for work disability, also provide injured workers with an additional benefit that is designed to compensate for noneconomic loss (or nonwork disability). The examples we focus on here are the "permanent impairment" benefits in Florida that were available from 1979 to 1993 and the "noneconomic loss" benefits that have been paid in Ontario, Canada, since 1990. The operational basis for the noneconomic loss benefits in both Florida and Ontario corresponds to the "pure" permanent impairment approach (see Table A.1).

In both jurisdictions, the primary basis for assessment has been the *AMA Guides* (American Medical Association, 2000). When the noneconomic loss benefits program was still in existence in Florida, reliance on the *AMA Guides* was challenged in a number of court cases. Research by Sinclair and Burton (1995, pp. 123–140) on noneconomic loss benefits in Ontario raises serious doubts about the appropriateness of using the *AMA Guides'* permanent impairment ratings as a proxy for the extent of noneconomic loss. Despite these problems with the operational approach for noneconomic loss that depends on an assessment of the extent of an impairment and/or functional limitations, we are unaware of any other operational approach used by U.S. or Canadian jurisdictions (in addition to Florida and Ontario) that currently provides, or that once provided, PPD benefits for noneconomic loss.

Distinctions Among Injuries and Diseases

All jurisdictions have different PPD benefits (measured by weekly amount or potential duration) for different categories of injuries and diseases, and some jurisdictions use different operational approaches for different categories of injuries. The three most common types of distinctions that jurisdictions make are the following: distinctions between diseases and injuries, distinctions among various types of injuries, and distinctions among injuries with differing severity levels.

Several states provide more restrictive PPD benefits for diseases than for injuries (U.S. Chamber of Commerce, 2003, Chart IV). Montana, for example, does not provide compensation for partial disability resulting from a disease. In Idaho and South Dakota, partial disability resulting from silicosis is not compensable. In Iowa, partial disability rated at less than 33-1/3 percent is not compensable if the cause is pneumoconiosis, and Ohio does not provide partial disability benefits for respiratory dust disease.

With regard to different types of injuries, most states treat "scheduled" injuries differently from "nonscheduled" injuries. A *scheduled injury* is any injury that is specifically enumerated in the workers' compensation statute; scheduled injuries typically involve injuries to the upper and lower extremities (arms, legs, hands, feet, fingers, and toes). In addition, states commonly schedule benefits for the enucleation of an eye and for hearing and vision loss. Injuries to the trunk, back, internal organs (such as heart or lungs), nervous system, and other body systems usually are not specified in the list of injuries found in the statutes; these are *nonscheduled injuries*. In some states, they are referred to as "unscheduled" injuries. We describe these states as the "scheduled/nonscheduled distinction states." However, these terms are not used by jurisdictions in a uniform and unambiguous fashion. The workers' compensation statutes in most states contain a schedule that lists the number of weeks or the dollar amounts of compensation benefits to be paid for the physical loss or (in most states) the loss of the use of specified parts of the body.

A significant minority of states does not distinguish between "scheduled" injuries and "nonscheduled" injuries in the way that was just defined. These "unitary rating system states" either specify by statute that a particular rating system should be used for all injuries, or the statute authorizes the workers' compensation agency to adopt a comprehensive rating system. In California, all permanent disabilities are rated according to a schedule that is unique to California.

Finally, regarding PPD benefits, many jurisdictions provide more generous benefits (in terms of weekly amount and/or potential duration) for more serious injuries than for less serious injuries. Some states also distinguish between injuries that result in amputation of a body member and injuries that involve permanent loss of use of a body member. Workers with the former injury may be entitled to PPD benefits, while those with the latter injury may not.

PPD Benefits Systems Used in North America

The U.S. states and Canadian provinces utilize the three operational approaches (see Table A.1) to determine work disability benefits and the one operational approach to determine nonwork disability benefits within a variety of PPD benefits systems. Each jurisdiction has its own "system" of PPD benefits because, without exception, each jurisdiction makes some distinction among the types of injuries or diseases that affects either the operational approach for determining the benefits or the amount or duration of those benefits. This section describes six systems of PPD benefits, each of which is used in at least one North American jurisdiction. Some states do not neatly fit into one of the six systems, but we believe the following taxonomy provides a good representation of the most important or interesting PPD benefits systems.[4] We begin with three systems of PPD benefits used in the scheduled/nonscheduled distinction states.

System 1: Scheduled/Nonscheduled Permanent Impairment Approach for Nonscheduled Injuries

Most states have PPD benefits systems that distinguish between scheduled and nonscheduled injuries. In about a dozen states that rely on this distinction, both scheduled and nonscheduled injuries receive PPD benefits based on the extent of permanent impairment.

Indiana and Washington rely on the "pure" permanent impairment approach (see Table A.1) for both scheduled and nonscheduled injuries. In Washington, benefits for scheduled losses are based on impairment and do not vary with the worker's wage. As of 2003, for example, the loss of a hand was valued at $80,522. A worker who experienced an injury to the hand that resulted in a permanent impairment rating of 50 percent would receive $40,261 in PPD benefits. Likewise, nonscheduled injuries (such as back injuries) were rated relative to a total-body impairment, which

---

[4] The six systems of PPD benefits were identified by John Burton in 2004 for this study and were based in part on Burton (1996). Burton assigned the states to the six categories largely based on the descriptions of PPD benefits in Barth and Niss (1999). However, some states, e.g., Arizona and New York, are classified differently by Barth and Niss than they are in our taxonomy.

had a value of $149,116 in 2003 and did not vary with the worker's pre-injury wage. Thus, a worker in Washington whose back was rated with a 20 percent permanent impairment would receive $29,823.[5]

A more common approach, used in some states,[6] is to rely on the Permanent Impairment and Pre-Injury Wage approach for both scheduled and nonscheduled injuries (see Table A.1). In those states, a worker who suffers the physical loss or loss of use of a part of the body included in the schedule is evaluated in terms of the seriousness of the impairment, and the rating is used to determine the duration of the benefits. In New Jersey—which equates the loss of an arm with 330 weeks of benefits and which provides an extra 15 percent to the rating if the injury results in an amputation—a worker who loses the use of half an arm is entitled to 189.75 weeks of benefits ($330 \times 0.5 \times 1.15$). An injury that leads to the loss of use of a body part listed in the schedule is evaluated in terms of the extent of the functional limitations that result from that loss. Thus, in New Jersey—which equates the loss of a hand with 245 weeks of benefits—a worker with an injury that causes a 20 percent loss of the use of a hand will receive 49 weeks of benefits (245×0.2). Most states (including New Jersey) pay scheduled benefits if a worker experiences either a physical loss or a loss of use of a body part listed in the schedule, but a few states (such as Michigan) pay only scheduled benefits for amputations. The weekly benefit for scheduled PPD benefits in New Jersey is 70 percent of a worker's pre-injury wage, subject to maximum weekly amounts that depend on the number of weeks of PPD benefits.

In the states (such as New Jersey) that use the Permanent Impairment and Pre-Injury Wage approach for scheduled PPD benefits, nonscheduled injuries also receive PPD benefits based on the extent of impairment or functional limitations and the worker's pre-injury wage.[7] For example, a worker may experience structural damage to a vertebra and the spinal column, which is an injury not found on the schedule. The impairment itself may be evaluated (e.g., the disc is herniated) or the consequent functional limitation may be assessed (e.g., the worker's ability to lift, stoop, or per-

---

[5] The benefit amounts cited in this appendix are based on Hallmark (2003), unless otherwise indicated.

[6] The states that appear to belong in this category are Delaware, Georgia, New Jersey, Oklahoma, South Dakota, Utah, and West Virginia. Colorado may also belong in this category, although the fit is not perfect because Barth and Niss (1999) indicate that the duration of the unscheduled benefits in Colorado has a small adjustment factor for age.

[7] New Jersey is offered as an example of a state that relies on the impairment approach in determining the rating for nonscheduled permanent partial disability benefits. This categorization of New Jersey can be justified using an analysis by the National Council on Compensation Insurance (1995, p. 31), which identifies New Jersey as a state in which "weeks payable [are] related to impairment rating of the whole person" for nonscheduled benefits. In practice, the distinction between the permanent impairment approach and the loss of earning capacity approach is not always clear. Berkowitz and Burton (1987, p. 137) described the rating process in New Jersey as follows: "The judge is informed by the petitioner about complaints, and his evaluation of these complaints may well influence where, in the range, the decision will be. Such complaints may well involve the claimant's evaluation of his poor employment prospects. The judge may evaluate such information in light of the petitioner's age, occupation, and possibly even the effects of the injury on the nonwork activities of the claimant."

form certain motions is restricted when compared with his or her ability to do so before the injury). This approach to nonscheduled injuries produces a percentage rating that relates the worker's condition to that of a whole person (or to a "totally disabled" person). Thus, in New Jersey, the statute equates a whole person to 600 weeks of PPD benefits, and a worker with an impairment rating of 25 percent would receive 150 weeks of PPD benefits. The weekly amount for unscheduled PPD benefits in New Jersey is 70 percent of the worker's pre-injury wage, subject to maximum weekly amounts that depend on the number of weeks of PPD benefits.

System 2: Scheduled/Nonscheduled, Loss of Earning Capacity Approach for Nonscheduled Injuries

This system for PPD benefits draws a distinction between scheduled and nonscheduled injuries similar to that found in System 1.[8] The scheduled injuries in System 2 are compensated on the basis of the permanent impairment. The distinctive feature of System 2 is that the nonscheduled benefits are based on the LEC approach (see Table A.1).

Four states (Iowa, Maryland, Mississippi, and Nebraska) use the Permanent Impairment and Pre-Injury Wage approach for scheduled injuries and the "Ad Hoc" Loss of Earning Capacity approach (see Table A.1) for nonscheduled injuries. Two states (Idaho and Oregon) use the "Pure" Permanent Impairment approach for scheduled injuries. In Oregon, for example, each body part in the schedule is assigned a number of degrees of impairment (to a maximum of 320 degrees). As of January 2003, each degree was valued at $454. The loss of a hand is a 150-degree impairment that had a value of $83,850 in 2003. The nonscheduled PPD benefits in these two states are based on the "Pure" Loss of Earning Capacity approach. In Idaho, for example, the LEC is determined by assessing the degree of permanent impairment and the worker's age, education, and labor-market prospects. The duration of the nonscheduled PPD benefits is 500 weeks times the LEC rating. The weekly benefit for all workers is set at 55 percent of the state's average weekly wage.

Several states (Alabama, Arkansas, Kansas, North Carolina, and Wisconsin) rely on the impairment approach for scheduled benefits and on what Barth and Niss (1999) labeled a "bifurcated" system with two tracks of nonscheduled benefits, at least one of which relies on the loss of earning capacity approach.[9] Wisconsin relies

---

[8] The distinction between scheduled and nonscheduled injuries in Wisconsin is similar to that in New Jersey, with injuries to arms, legs, hands, and other extremities listed in the statutory schedule and injuries to the back and internal organs not listed. The scheduled benefit durations in the two jurisdictions differ, however. An injury to an arm, for example, is worth 500 weeks of benefits in Wisconsin compared with 330 weeks of benefits in New Jersey.

[9] Bifurcated benefit systems in which one of the tracks of nonscheduled benefits involves wage-loss benefits are discussed later in this appendix.

on the Permanent Impairment and Pre-Injury Wage approach for scheduled injuries. For nonscheduled injuries, there are the following two possibilities.

If the worker has returned to work and is earning at least 85 percent of his or her pre-injury wage, the worker's PI is rated. The duration of PPD benefits for such a worker is determined by multiplying the PI rating by 1,000 weeks. The weekly benefit is two-thirds of the worker's pre-injury wage, subject to a maximum benefit of $222 per week. Thus, the Wisconsin PPD benefits for the worker who has returned to work and is earning at least 85 percent of his or her pre-injury wages are based on the Permanent Impairment and Pre-Injury Wage approach.

If a worker in Wisconsin with a nonscheduled injury has not returned to work or has returned to work but is not earning at least 85 percent of his or her pre-injury wage, the worker's loss of earning capacity is determined. The evaluation of the LEC takes into account the seriousness of the worker's permanent impairment plus such factors as the worker's age, education, and prior work experience. The evaluation produces a rating indicating the percentage loss in earning capacity due to the injury. The statute equates full earning capacity to a specified duration, which in Wisconsin is 1,000 weeks. Thus, a Wisconsin worker with a 25 percent loss of earning capacity would receive 250 weeks of PPD benefits. The weekly benefit is two-thirds of the worker's pre-injury wage, subject to a maximum benefit of $222 per week. Thus, the nonscheduled PPD benefits for Wisconsin workers who have not returned to work or have returned to work but are not earning at least 85 percent of their pre-injury wages are based on the "Ad Hoc" Loss of Earning Capacity approach (see Table A.1).

System 3: Scheduled/Nonscheduled, Actual Wage Loss Approach for Nonscheduled Injuries

This system draws a distinction between scheduled and nonscheduled injuries similar to that found in Systems 1 and 2. And, similar to Systems 1 and 2, the scheduled injuries in System 3 are compensated on the basis of the permanent impairment. The distinctive feature of this system is that the nonscheduled benefits are based on the actual wage loss approach.

Six jurisdictions provide PPD benefits using System 3.[10] The first step in System 3 in determining the applicable benefits for an injury with permanent consequences is to determine whether the injury is scheduled or unscheduled. The distinction is similar to that used in New Jersey and Wisconsin, in which injuries to arms, legs, and other bodily extremities are classified as scheduled injuries, and injuries to internal organs and the back are defined as unscheduled injuries.[11] In New York, the

---

[10] The six are the District of Columbia, Louisiana, Maine, Michigan, New York, and Pennsylvania. Barth and Niss (1999) also include Arizona in this category.

[11] The scheduled durations of benefits differ among the states; in New York, an arm is worth only 312 weeks of benefits.

operational basis for scheduled PPD benefits is the Permanent Impairment and Pre-Injury Wage approach.

While all the traits of the actual wage loss approach cannot be covered in this appendix,[12] several are worth emphasizing here, albeit in an abbreviated form; their counterparts in New York's system of providing nonscheduled benefits are noted. One trait of the AWL approach is that, unless the worker has actual earnings after the date of MMI that are less than the worker's pre-injury earnings, no benefits are paid even if the work injury has resulted in a permanent impairment or loss of earning capacity. This is a crucial difference between the actual wage-loss approach and the loss of earning capacity approach—a worker who experiences a loss of earning capacity but has no actual loss of earnings is precluded from benefits in the wage-loss approach but is *not* precluded from benefits in the loss of earning capacity approach.

Another characteristic of the AWL approach is that the total duration of the PPD benefits is *not* determined shortly after the date of MMI, as in the PI or LEC approaches. Instead, the duration of benefits depends on the length of time the worker experiences actual losses of earnings due to the work injury. In New York, this duration can range from zero weeks (for those cases closed with no present wage loss) to the balance of the worker's life.

There are three possible outcomes for nonscheduled injuries in New York:

1. If, at the time the case is initially classified as a nonscheduled PPD, the worker has returned to work and is experiencing no wage loss, the worker receives no PPD benefits and the case is closed.
2. If, at the time the case is initially classified as a nonscheduled PPD, the worker experiences a wage loss, benefits commence. The length of time these benefits will continue is unknown because the duration of subsequent wage loss is unknown. The exact variant of the AWL approach depends on whether the worker has any earnings during the permanent disability period.[13] If the worker has some earnings, then the "Pure" Actual Wage Loss approach is used. Thus, if a worker had pre-injury wages of $500 per week and returns to employment at $200 per week, the nonscheduled benefits is two-thirds of the wage loss, which means that the weekly benefit is $200. (The weekly PPD benefit is subject to a maximum of $400 per week.) If the worker does not have any earnings in the permanent disability period, then the Limited Actual Wage Loss approach (see Table A.1) is used. The worker's loss of earning capacity is evaluated and serves as a limit on the worker's wage loss. Thus, if a worker had pre-injury wages of $400, does not return to work, and is rated as having a 50 percent loss of earning capacity, and

---

[12] For a more detailed discussion of the wage loss approach, see Berkowitz and Burton (1987).

[13] This discussion of what happens if the worker had any earnings during the permanent disability period is based on Berkowitz and Burton (1987).

the nonscheduled benefits are two-thirds of the wage loss, the weekly PPD benefit is $133.33 ($400 × 0.5 × 0.667).

The worker's eligibility for nonscheduled benefits, as well as the weekly amount of those benefits, can change through time in jurisdictions using the AWL approach. For example, in New York, a worker whose case is initially closed with no benefits due to a lack of present wage loss can reopen the case for up to 18 years after the date of injury or eight years after the last benefit payment. PPD benefits can commence after the reopening of the case if the work injury is then causing lost earnings. This approach can be described as a *retrospective* or *ex post* approach to PPD benefits, because the amount and duration of PPD benefits are not known until the period of permanent disability is over (or the period for reopening a case has expired).

3. A lump-sum settlement is the third outcome for a nonscheduled PPD case in New York. This settlement is essentially a compromise and release (C&R) agreement in which the parties reach a compromise concerning the amount of benefits to be paid, the worker receives a lump-sum payment, and the employer is released from any further liability for the particular injury.[14]

System 4: Unitary Rating System, Single Operational Approach for Benefits

The three PPD benefit systems listed above all rely on a distinction between scheduled injuries (those specifically listed in the workers' compensation statute) and unscheduled injuries (those not listed in the statute). States using Systems 4 and 5 are unitary rating system states in which all injuries are evaluated using the same operational approach (System 4) or the same set of operational approaches (System 5).

California is an example of a jurisdiction providing System 4 PPD benefits, in which all injuries are rated using the same approach. California relies on a formula to combine the impairment ratings with age and occupational factors to produce a disability rating, which describes the Loss of Earning Capacity by Formula approach (see Table A.1). Other unitary rating system states that rate all injuries using this approach are Nevada and Wyoming.[15]

The system that California uses to assign disability ratings is discussed in detail in Chapter Three. The California PPD system uses the disability rating to determine the duration of PPD benefits. It uses a formula that provides more weeks of benefits per each percent of disability rating for serious injuries than for less-than-serious injuries. In the version of the formula that was in effect between January 1, 1992, and

---

[14] The use of C&R agreements in the New York workers' compensation program is examined in Thomason and Burton (1993).

[15] In addition to the three states with unitary rating systems that rely on the Loss of Earning Capacity by Formula approach for all injuries, Alaska and Minnesota have unitary rating systems that rely on the "Pure" Permanent Impairment approach for all injuries.

December 31, 2003, each percent of disability rating under 10 percent received three weeks of PPD benefits; each percent of disability rating between 10 and 19.75 percent received four weeks of benefits; each percent of disability rating between 20 and 24.75 percent received five weeks of benefits; and so on (Hannigan and Swezey, 2003, Section 5.7). For example, a worker with a disability rating of 64 percent was entitled to 378.25 weeks of benefits using the 1992–2003 formula. Effective January 1, 2004, the formula was modified so that the two lowest categories received an extra week of benefits—for example, each percent of disability rating under 10 percent received four weeks of benefits. Further changes have been made under SB 899.

The California PPD benefits system draws a distinction among workers depending on the magnitude of the disability rating. A disability rating of 100 percent qualifies a worker for permanent total disability benefits for life. A disability rating between 1 percent and 69.75 percent qualifies a worker for PPD benefits. A worker with a disability rating between 70 percent and 99.75 percent qualifies for PPD benefits using the formula summarized above, and when those PPD benefits expire, the worker qualifies for a life pension.[16]

System 5: The Hybrid Approach

The fifth noteworthy system of PPD benefits is the hybrid approach, which potentially pays two types of PPD benefits on a sequential basis. This approach is used in Connecticut and Texas and was used in Florida between 1994 and 2003.[17]

Consider the approach used in Florida from 1994 to 2003. The initial phase of PPD benefits was based on the Permanent Impairment and Pre-Injury Wage approach. After the worker reached the date of MMI (or, in the case of a worker still receiving TTD benefits, six weeks prior to the maximum duration of 104 weeks), the extent of permanent impairment for all injuries with permanent consequences was rated using the *AMA Guides* or Florida's own impairment schedule. Three weeks of impairment benefits were then paid for each 1 percent impairment rating. The weekly benefits were 50 percent of the worker's average TTD benefit.

Those workers who had a permanent impairment rating of at least 20 percent had an opportunity to qualify for wage-loss benefits after the impairment benefits expired (i.e., at least 60 weeks after the initial eligibility date for impairment benefits). The wage-loss benefits were paid to workers who experience at least a 20 percent drop in wages between the pre-injury period and the period of permanent dis-

---

[16] The *life pension* is a weekly benefit that is 1.5 percent of the worker's pre-injury wage for each 1 percent of disability over 60 percent, subject to a maximum weekly benefit (Hannigan and Swezey, 2003, Section 5.9).

[17] Texas and Florida use the Permanent Impairment approach and Pre-Injury Wage approach for the initial phase of their PPD benefits and the Limited Actual Wage Loss approach for the second phase of their PPD benefits. Connecticut uses the Permanent Impairment approach and Pre-Injury Wage approach for the initial phase of its PPD benefits and the "Pure" Actual Wage Loss approach for the second phase of its PPD benefits.

ability; 80 percent of the wage loss in excess of the 20 percent threshold was compensated. The wage-loss benefits in Florida are an example of the Limited Actual Wage Loss approach.

System 6: The Dual Benefits Approach

A few jurisdictions have explicitly paid nonwork disability (or noneconomic loss) benefits in addition to work disability benefits. The System 6 dual PPD benefits approach was used in Florida from 1979 until 1993, although some significant modifications were made in 1990 prior to the total abandonment of the approach in 1993.

There were two types of benefits under the dual benefits approach— impairment benefits and wage loss benefits—and an injured worker with permanent consequences from his or her injury could qualify for either, both,[18] or neither of the benefits, depending on the facts of the case.

Impairment benefits were paid to workers with certain types of permanent impairments, including amputations, loss of 80 percent or more of vision, or serious head or facial disfigurements. Other types of permanent impairments, such as total or partial loss of the use of a body member without amputation, did not qualify for the benefits. The specified impairments were to be rated using an appropriate rating system. The permanent impairment ratings were translated into a total dollar amount using a formula that varied through time: The initial 1979 legislation provided $50 for each percent of permanent impairment for ratings of 1 percent to 50 percent and $100 for each percent over 50 percent. Thus, a worker with a 60 percent impairment rating received $3,500 under the 1979 law. The purpose of these "impairment benefits" was to compensate the worker for nonwork disability. The impairment benefits were paid using the "Pure" Permanent Impairment approach.

The wage loss benefits contained in the 1979 Florida legislation required a worker to have at least a 1 percent permanent impairment rating. In addition, the worker had to experience at least a 15 percent decline from the wages in the pre-injury period to the wages in the permanent disability period. The wage loss benefits then replaced 95 percent of the actual wage loss in excess of the 15 percent threshold. The 1979 law provided that the maximum duration for the wage loss benefits was 350 weeks. This duration was first extended and then contracted during the 1979–1993 reign of the dual benefits approach in Florida.

This description of the dual benefits approach in Florida is simplistic and does not capture the initial acclaim and eventual disillusionment with the approach, especially the wage loss component, which ultimately led to the abandonment of the dual

---

[18] The possibility that a worker with a single injury could receive both impairment benefits and wage loss benefits differs from the System 1, 2, and 3 PPD benefits, in which a worker with a single injury qualifies for either scheduled or nonscheduled benefits. There are occasional exceptions to this statement in regard to System 1 and System 2 benefits, such as a scheduled injury that has psychological "overlays" that are nonscheduled.

benefits approach in Florida after 1993. However, we would be remiss in this overview of operational approaches to PPD benefits systems in North America if we did not mention that the dual benefits approach is still alive and apparently operating well in several Canadian provinces, including Ontario and Saskatchewan.

Summary

We identified three operational approaches for work disability benefits that are used in the PPD benefits systems in the U.S. and Canadian workers' compensation programs: (1) the permanent impairment approach, in which benefits are based on the extent of impairment and/or functional limitation; (2) the loss of earning capacity approach, in which benefits are based on the extent of loss of earning capacity; and (3) the actual wage loss approach, in which benefits are based on the extent of actual wage loss. We also identified variations on these three operational approaches and one operational approach for nonwork disability benefits that was used in the PPD benefit system in Florida and is still widely used in Canadian workers' compensation programs, which bases benefits on the extent of impairment and/or functional limitation.

These operational approaches are building blocks that can be used to construct an almost unlimited number of systems for PPD benefits. This appendix identified six different PPD benefits systems, and others are possible. Several observations on the six systems discussed in this appendix are warranted, which draw in part on a survey of state PPD programs by Barth and Niss (1999).

- First, the most common type of system appears to be System 1, in which both scheduled and nonscheduled benefits are based on the permanent impairment approach. Barth and Niss (1999) reported that about 13 jurisdictions use this approach.[19]
- Second, Systems 3 and 4, which contain elements of the AWL approach in which benefits begin for some types of injuries at the date of MMI, appear to be threatened, at least in the United States. Florida has abandoned the dual benefits system (System 6), and Pennsylvania, which has used a variant of System 3 (in which scheduled benefits are based on the PI approach, and nonscheduled

---

[19] The National Council on Compensation Insurance (1995) indicated that of the 42 jurisdictions (including the District of Columbia) in which certain permanent partial injuries were compensated on a nonscheduled basis, eight jurisdictions (including the District of Columbia) used the AWL approach, 26 states used the PI approach, and 14 states used some other approach (in most cases, probably the LEC approach). (Some states fell into more than one category.) Burton (1995) argued that Arizona is actually a loss of earning capacity state (not a wage loss state) and New York is actually a wage loss state (not an "other" state). However, these misclassifications should not affect the conclusion that the System 1 version of PPD benefits, in which the PI approach is used for nonscheduled benefits, is the most common system.

benefits are based on the AWL approach),[20] has recently added a qualification that benefits can be reduced, even if a worker does not have actual earnings in the permanent disability period, so long as the employer can establish that light-duty work is available within commuting distance.[21]

- Third, use of System 5, the hybrid approach, has attracted some interest in recent decades. Florida adopted this approach in 1994, only to abandon it in 2003. The current Connecticut and Texas statutes provide impairment income benefits followed by supplemental income benefits.

- Fourth, we want to emphasize a critical distinction between (1) the permanent impairment operational approach and the loss of earning capacity approach and (2) the actual wage loss approach. The states that rely on the actual wage loss approach require a worker to demonstrate (1) that a work-related injury has produced a permanent impairment and/or loss of earning capacity[22] and (2) that he or she has experienced an actual loss of earnings because of the work-related injury or disease. In contrast, the PI and LEC approaches will pay PPD benefits even if there is no actual loss of earnings, so long as the worker can demonstrate that the work injury caused a diminution in one of the proxies for actual wage loss.

- Finally, C&R agreements, in which workers release their claim to future benefits in exchange for a lump-sum settlement, can turn the AWL approach (in which the amount of the PPD benefits is unknown until the end of the period of permanent disability or the worker reaches the statutory maximum for such benefits) into the loss of earning capacity approach (in which the amount of PPD benefits is determined near the beginning of the period of permanent disability based on an assessment of the extent of loss of earning capacity).

---

[20] Pennsylvania's PPD benefits are described in Berkowitz and Burton (1987, Chapter 8).

[21] For a report on recent reforms of the Pennsylvania workers' compensation law, see Bureau of National Affairs (1996).

[22] States differ on which of the permanent consequences (permanent impairment, functional limitations, or loss of earning capacity) must be demonstrated, and differ also on the extent of the consequences that is required for wage loss benefits to be paid.

Further Discussion of the Correlation Among Disability Ratings, Benefits, and Earnings Losses

Disability Ratings and Causal Influences on Earnings Losses

A key assumption underlying our analysis in Chapter Five is that the positive relationship between observed earnings losses and disability ratings is driven by higher-rated claims for more-severe impairments. If higher disability ratings influenced the behavior of injured workers in such a way that higher ratings led to inflated earnings losses, our evaluation would be confounded. One reason we might worry about this kind of blurred causality between losses and disability ratings is that higher disability ratings lead to higher benefits. If the higher benefits induced injured workers to reduce their labor supply, then this reduction could generate a positive relationship between losses and ratings, such as seen in Figure 5.5, regardless of the true relationship between functional limitations, ratings, and loss of earnings capacity.

Permanent disability benefits act as an increase in wealth to recipients, because one can work and still receive PPD benefits.[1] There have been numerous studies that have estimated the responsiveness of labor supply to changes in wealth, with the general consensus being that wealth shocks have a persistent but fairly small impact on both earnings and labor force participation.[2] A full accounting of the relationship between ratings and earnings losses that we observe in Figures 5.3 and 5.5 is beyond the scope of this report, but we can show that we would require very high wealth elasticities, probably unreasonably high, of labor supply for our results in Chapter Five to be explained solely by reverse causality of benefits on losses.

Consider Figure B.1, which illustrates, by injury severity in our sample, the effect of disability on labor force participation. The figure shows the fraction of workers that report some earnings three years after injury (i.e., in quarter 12). The gray

---

[1] We distinguish "wealth" from "income" in the sense that an individual earns income in the labor market, while wealth is anything that is not earned in the labor market by that individual. By this definition, one's own earnings in the labor market would be considered income, but one's spouse's earnings would be considered wealth.

[2] For extensive surveys of the literature, see Killingsworth and Heckman (1986), Pencavel (1986), Heckman (1993), Blundell and MaCurdy (1999), and Imbens, Rubin, and Sacerdote (2001).

Figure B.1
Employment of Injured Workers and Control Workers by Final Disability Rating

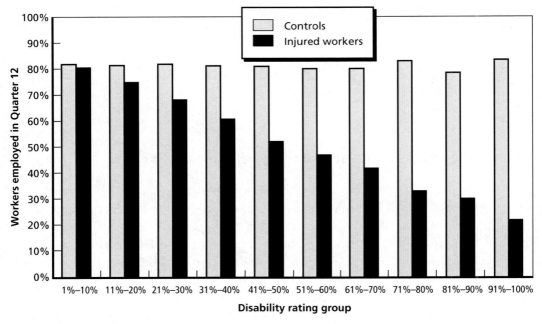

bars represent the fraction of control workers employed in quarter 12 for each rating group, while the black bars represent the fraction of injured workers employed in quarter 12.[3]

Figure B.1 shows that the average percentage of employment of control workers in quarter 12 is very high, close to 80 percent for all disability ratings.[4] Injured workers, however, show a clear trend in declining labor force participation for higher-rated injuries. Approximately 75 percent of workers with injuries rated between 11 and 20 percent are employed in quarter 12, about a –6.5 percentage point difference from the employment of the control workers. Only about 47 percent of injured workers with injuries rated between 51 and 60 percent are employed in quarter 12, a –33 percentage point difference from the control workers. More generally, the percentage of injured workers working in quarter 12 declines with each successive rating group.

---

[3] Recall that the "control" workers, as stated earlier, are workers who were similar to the injured workers with respect to economic characteristics, but who did not experience a workplace injury during the time period under examination.

[4] Because control workers do not experience injuries, they do not have disability ratings. The controls are ranked based on the disability ratings received by the injured workers with which they are associated.

Figure B.1 indicates a very clear correlation between disability ratings and the employment of injured workers. The question that concerns us is, how much of that correlation could plausibly be driven by the higher workers' compensation benefits given to the workers with higher final ratings? While we cannot address this question directly, we can examine the increase in benefits associated with higher ratings and estimate how strong a wealth elasticity of labor supply would be needed to generate the correlation displayed in the figure. If we find that these implied elasticities are significantly higher than those estimated in the literature, it would suggest that the close association between ratings and earnings losses that we observe is real.

In Table B.1, we show the observed employment outcomes and estimated indemnity benefits for the injured workers in our sample. Our data do not include any information on the actual benefits paid to workers, so we estimate the benefits based on the disability rating. We assume that the injured workers have wages high enough to earn the maximum PPD benefit, which is true for more than 60 percent of our sample, and we use the schedule that was in effect for injuries occurring on or after July 1, 1996.[5] Benefits are calculated using the midpoint of each range—e.g., the benefits for the 11–20 percent rating category were calculated as if the final rating were 15.

Table B.1
Employment, Benefits, and Implied Labor-Supply Elasticities, for Injured Workers in Sample

Final Rating (Percent)	Difference in Labor Force Participation[a]	Percentage Change in Labor Force Participation	Estimated Disability Benefits	Percentage Change in Benefits	Implied $|\eta|$ Wealth Elasticity
1–10	−0.013		$2,100		
11–20	−0.065	−395	$8,040	283	1.40
21–30	−0.136	−109	$16,278	102	1.07
31–40	−0.204	−50	$27,370	68	0.73
41–50	−0.286	−40	$39,270	43	0.93
51–60	−0.330	−15	$52,063	33	0.46
61–70	−0.380	−15	$65,663	26	0.58
71–80	−0.495	−30	$108,445	65	0.47
81–90	−0.477	4	$129,145	19	0.19
91–100	−0.611	−28	$149,845	16	1.75

[a]The number 0.000 in this column would be a benchmark (i.e., the disabled would have the same workforce participation as the controls); the number −1.000 would mean that all control workers were working, and no disabled workers were working.

---

[5] Our use of this schedule is a conservative one, because the earlier disability schedules that are applicable to injuries in our sample had similar benefits for low-rated injuries but higher benefits for high-rated injuries. By increasing the variation in benefits between ratings groups, we are implicitly adding a downward bias to our imputed labor supply elasticities.

The second column of Table B.1 shows the difference in labor force participation between control workers and injured workers for each disability-rating category. As was seen in Figure 5.5, these differences are quite large, especially for the more serious disabilities. The fourth column of the table displays the estimated disability benefits for each disability category. For most injuries, indemnity benefits are fairly small. As mentioned in Chapter Five, 84 percent of injured workers have a disability rating below 40 percent, implying that for a vast majority of cases, the total benefits are less than $27,370. Nevertheless, for the highest ratings, we see that indemnity benefits can be substantial, with the benefits for the 91 to 100 group equaling $149,845.

The third and fifth columns of Table B.1 present the percentage changes in differential labor force participation and benefits, respectively, for the disability rating categories. We can use these numbers to impute the wealth elasticity of the labor supply that would be required to explain the observed decline in labor force participation if the decline were driven *entirely* by higher workers' compensation indemnity benefits. Wealth elasticity, denoted as η, can be defined as the percentage drop in labor force participation due to a 1 percent increase in wealth, i.e.,

$$\eta = \frac{\%\Delta L}{\%\Delta B}.$$

The absolute value of these implied labor supply elasticities are reported in the sixth column of Table B.1. Unfortunately, the range of results of past studies tends to be too wide to say whether these implied elasticities are "too strong," although many of the very high elasticities are thought to result more from tenuous specifications (Heckman, 1993). The elasticities shown in Table B.1 are considerably more negative than the elasticities found in studies that focus on a randomized treatment design, such as the Negative Income Tax (NIT) experiments or lotteries, in which the elasticities have tended to range from 0 to −0.25 (Imbens, Rubin, and Sacerdote, 2001). The elasticities are particularly high for the lower-rated cases in our sample, which is where most of the observations are found. Thus, for the majority of our sample, the role of disability benefits in driving the cross-impairment differences in earnings losses is probably negligible.

One limitation of this approach is that we have no data on medical payments or vocational rehabilitation benefits. Medical payments should, in theory, be earmarked toward medical expenditures and thus have no effect on labor supply. In practice, payments for medical expenditures may be settled upon and paid to injured workers as cash, so it could have an impact on labor supply. To the extent that these payments for medical expenditures are based on the size of the disability rating, we would overestimate the size of the implied labor elasticity.

The impact of disability benefits on labor force participation is only one reason we might worry that the disability ratings themselves, as opposed to actual severity of impairment, drive proportional losses. Another, perhaps more serious, concern is that the process of obtaining higher disability ratings leads to higher earnings losses. The permanent disability system in California has the reputation of being particularly contentious and litigious. Prolonged battles over high disability ratings may put stress on the employee-employer relationship to the point that the employee's long-term economic outcomes suffer. If the long-term economic outcomes were affected, then the positive correlation observed between earnings losses and ratings would reflect this tension between workers and employers (and confound our estimate of the relationship between ratings and disability severity).

One way to study the extent of this problem is to focus on the earnings losses of injured workers who continue to work. Earnings losses can be driven by either reduced labor force participation or lower wages, or some combination of the two. If earnings losses are actually driven by the process of determining disability ratings, we would expect to see reduced labor force participation rather than lower earnings for those who work. Lower earnings losses for injured workers who continue to work more likely are due to reduced working hours and lower marginal productivity due to the disability. If we observe a similar positive correlation between losses and disability ratings for workers who are working, this correlation should alleviate some concerns about the endogeneity of earnings losses.

Figure B.2 illustrates the correlation between proportional earnings losses and disability ratings, both unconditionally and conditionally on working. What we call unconditional losses are illustrated in Figure 5.5. The proportional losses conditional on working are calculated using a technique that Peterson et al. (1997) refer to as "Method I" (the approach used in this report up until now is what they call "Method II"). The earnings of injured and control workers are included in the analysis only if both groups of workers are working (i.e., earnings for those workers are reported to the EDD). The conditional earnings losses can be thought of as a "conservative" or lower-bound estimate of earnings losses, because they ignore the impact of reduced labor force participation (which Figure B.1 shows can be quite significant).

From Figure B.2, we can see that while earnings losses conditional on working increase more slowly with increases in disability ratings than do unconditional losses, a clear positive correlation exists between losses conditional on working and unconditional losses. Relatively low-rated claims, having a 5 percent or lower rating, consistently have conditional losses under 5 percent. Claims with a rating between 30 and 35 percent, on the other hand, generally have losses at or above 10 percent. The conditional earnings losses are much lower, reflecting the fact that a significant portion of the adverse economic impact from disability can be explained by reduced labor force participation.

Figure B.2
Three-Year Cumulative Earnings Losses Conditional on Quarterly Employment Status

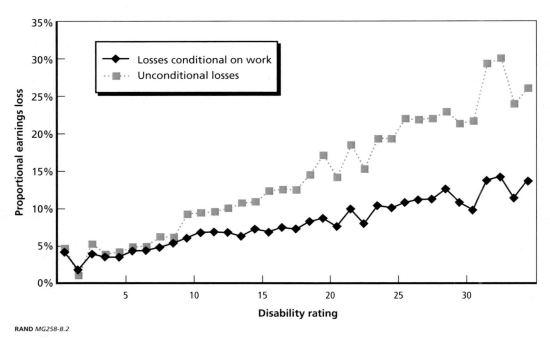

We cannot say with certainty the extent to which the positive relationship between ratings and earnings losses can be explained by the possible endogeneity of earnings losses to institutional processes tied to disability ratings. We can say, however, that reverse causality would need to be quite strong to explain away our results, stronger than what we generally believe is plausible (at least in terms of a labor supply effect). In particular, the fact that ratings are closely related to declines in the earnings of injured workers suggests that the ratings do measure some real decline in the productivity or employability of the disabled.

Derivation of the Adjustment Factor

A system that is horizontally equitable is one in which two impairments, A and B, with the same outcomes receive the same ratings. Formally, we can state this as follows:

$$E[r_A \mid wl^*] = E[r_B \mid wl^*],$$

where,

E[.] represents the expected value,

r_A is the final rating assigned to impairment A,

r_B is the final rating assigned to impairment B, and

wl^* represents some baseline level of proportional earnings losses.

Now, suppose initially that the average proportional earnings losses for A and B are identical, but the average disability ratings are not. In this case, we can adjust the ratings assigned to injury A by the factor

$$\theta = \frac{r_B}{r_A},$$

which will restore horizontal equity (because clearly $\theta r_A = r_B$).

Things are slightly more complicated if the average proportional losses are not equal—in other words, if the differences in ratings for claims of equal severity differed for high- and low-rated claims. In this case, the simple adjustment above would not be useful, because it would ignore possible differences in the average severity of impairments. To make adjustments that are consistent with impairment-level differences in severity, we need to incorporate differences in wage losses. We can do this with the following alternative adjustment,

$$\theta_2 = \frac{r_B}{r_A} \frac{wl_A}{wl_B},$$

where wl_A and wl_B represent the average proportional losses for impairments A and B, respectively. Now, if we adjust the rating assigned to impairment A using this second adjustment, we get the following:

$$\theta_2 r_A = r_B \frac{wl_A}{wl_B}.$$

Thus, if the average rating of impairment A is lower than that for impairment B, our adjustment sets the average rating for A to be equal to that for B scaled upward to account for the higher average proportional losses.

Nonlinear Reordering of the Schedule

In this section, we discuss the possibility of reordering the California rating schedule using earnings-loss data in a nonlinear fashion. In Chapter Five, we show how multipliers can be calculated for different impairment categories based on the disability ratings and estimated earnings losses. One concern, however, is that the relationship between losses and ratings might differ according to the size of the rating. If this were true, then the appropriate multiplier for a given impairment type with a low rating might be different from that for the same impairment type with a higher rating. Using Table B.2, we determine whether there appears to be any systematic nonlinearity in the appropriate modifier for single-disability, summary-rated claims.

The table presents average final ratings and proportional three-year earnings losses, and the ratio of the two, for the 14 single-impairment types discussed in Chapter Five. These variables are divided into disability rating quintiles for each impairment category. In other words, we order each impairment category by those falling below the 20th percentile (Q1), falling between the 20th and 40th percentiles (Q2), and so forth. And, for each group, we calculate the average final rating and three-year proportional earnings losses. Therefore, for a back impairment in the first quintile, the average final rating is 5 percent, and the average proportional losses are also 5 percent.[6]

Unfortunately, the information in the table provides little guidance on the systematic relationship between higher ratings and earnings losses. For the impairments that tend to have the lowest ratings relative to compensation (psychiatric and hearing), the relationship between ratings and proportional losses seems to converge to be close to one-to-one in the highest quintile (Q5). However, it is difficult to identify any discernable pattern for the other injuries.

Checking the Impact of Firm Size

In Chapter Five, we mentioned that the matching methodology we apply tends to lead to an oversampling of workers at medium-sized firms. For the purposes of this analysis, such oversampling would be of some concern if the relationship between earnings losses and disability ratings systematically differed for workers at different-sized firms. Past work has established that workers at smaller firms tend to suffer higher earnings losses (Reville et al., 2002b). This fact could cast some doubt on the findings noted here if workers at smaller firms also had higher ratings or, perhaps

---

[6] Note that, due to rounding, a ratio in the table may not exactly equal the ratio of the values for the rating and earnings losses.

more important, if they were more likely to have certain types of injuries than others. We briefly explore this issue here.

Table B.3 lists the average final disability ratings, proportional earnings losses, and distribution of injuries for workers in our sample at various-sized firms. We focus on only single-injury, summary-rated claims. We consider seven firm-size categories: 100 or fewer employees; 101 to 500 employees; 501 to 1,500 employees; 1,501 to 2,500 employees; 2,501 to 5,000 employees; 5,001 to 7,500 employees; and 7,500 employees or more. Approximately 25 percent of the observations in the table are for

Table B.2
Average Final Ratings, Three-Year Earnings Losses, and the Ratio of Ratings and Earnings Losses by Impairment Type and Rating Quintile

Impairment Type		Q1	Q2	Q3	Q4	Q5
Finger: One digit	Average final rating	0.01	0.02	0.03	0.04	0.10
	Proportional earnings losses	−0.02	0.02	0.04	0.03	0.04
		(0.03)	(0.04)	(0.04)	(0.03)	(0.04)
	$\dfrac{Avg.(Rate)}{Avg.(WL)}$	−0.49	1.23	0.85	1.38	2.57
Elbow	Average final rating	0.02	0.06	0.10	0.16	0.28
	Proportional earnings losses	−0.03	0.04	0.05	0.12	0.17
		(0.03)	(0.03)	(0.03)	(0.03)	(0.04)
	$\dfrac{Avg.(Rate)}{Avg.(WL)}$	−0.64	1.70	1.82	1.35	1.69
Knee	Average final rating	0.03	0.07	0.13	0.21	0.41
	Proportional earnings losses	0.01	0.04	0.06	0.11	0.25
		(0.01)	(0.01)	(0.02)	(0.02)	(0.02)
	$\dfrac{Avg.(Rate)}{Avg.(WL)}$	2.62	1.88	2.15	1.95	1.61
Ankle	Average final rating	0.03	0.06	0.12	0.21	0.44
	Proportional earnings losses	0.04	0.06	0.06	0.14	0.26
		(0.03)	(0.02)	(0.02)	(0.03)	(0.03)
	$\dfrac{Avg.(Rate)}{Avg.(WL)}$	0.67	1.05	2.04	1.48	1.68
Finger: Four digits	Average final rating	0.04	0.09	0.14	0.21	0.37
	Proportional earnings losses	0.02	0.09	0.03	0.12	0.30
		(0.05)	(0.05)	(0.07)	(0.06)	(0.07)
	$\dfrac{Avg.(Rate)}{Avg.(WL)}$	2.44	0.98	4.71	1.72	1.24
Loss of grasping power	Average final rating	0.04	0.07	0.11	0.17	0.33
	Proportional earnings losses	0.03	0.04	0.07	0.13	0.23
		(0.01)	(0.02)	(0.02)	(0.02)	(0.02)
	$\dfrac{Avg.(Rate)}{Avg.(WL)}$	1.34	1.95	1.53	1.29	1.44

Table B.2—Continued

Impairment Type		Q1	Q2	Q3	Q4	Q5
Wrist	Average final rating	0.03	0.07	0.13	0.2	0.38
	Proportional earnings losses	0.04 (0.02)	0.05 (0.03)	0.12 (0.02)	0.16 (0.03)	0.23 (0.03)
	$\frac{Avg.(Rate)}{Avg.(WL)}$	0.72	1.52	1.11	1.26	1.62
Back	Average final rating	0.05	0.12	0.18	0.27	0.45
	Proportional earnings losses	0.05 (0.01)	0.09 (0.01)	0.12 (0.01)	0.21 (0.01)	0.35 (0.01)
	$\frac{Avg.(Rate)}{Avg.(WL)}$	1.10	1.30	1.48	1.27	1.29
Finger: Five digits	Average final rating	0.04	0.09	0.14	0.2	0.38
	Proportional earnings losses	0.00 (0.05)	0.09 (0.04)	0.08 (0.04)	0.19 (0.04)	0.31 (0.05)
	$\frac{Avg.(Rate)}{Avg.(WL)}$	11.86	1.02	1.70	1.08	1.22
General upper extremity	Average final rating	0.05	0.12	0.18	0.26	0.45
	Proportional earnings losses	0.06 (0.02)	0.11 (0.02)	0.18 (0.02)	0.24 (0.02)	0.34 (0.03)
	$\frac{Avg.(Rate)}{Avg.(WL)}$	0.89	1.11	1.02	1.10	1.31
General lower extremity	Average final rating	0.03	0.08	0.17	0.27	0.53
	Proportional earnings losses	0.06 (0.06)	0.06 (0.05)	0.15 (0.05)	0.23 (0.05)	0.41 (0.05)
	$\frac{Avg.(Rate)}{Avg.(WL)}$	0.50	1.34	1.13	1.15	1.30
Shoulder	Average final rating	0.02	0.05	0.09	0.14	0.26
	Proportional earnings losses	0.03 (0.02)	0.06 (0.02)	0.10 (0.02)	0.17 (0.02)	0.28 (0.02)
	$\frac{Avg.(Rate)}{Avg.(WL)}$	0.77	0.85	0.86	0.85	0.93
Psychiatric	Average final rating	0.07	0.15	0.23	0.36	0.66
	Proportional earnings losses	0.37 (0.05)	0.43 (0.87)	0.46 (0.09)	0.55 (0.07)	0.65 (0.06)
	$\frac{Avg.(Rate)}{Avg.(WL)}$	0.19	0.35	0.50	0.66	1.01
Hearing	Average final rating	0.02	0.04	0.07	0.13	0.27
	Proportional earnings losses	0.18 (0.06)	0.19 (0.04)	0.22 (0.08)	0.25 (0.07)	0.26 (0.09)
	$\frac{Avg.(Rate)}{Avg.(WL)}$	0.11	0.21	0.32	0.53	1.05

NOTE: WL = wage loss.

workers at firms with more than 7,500 employees, the single largest category. About 32 percent of observations are for workers at firms with 500 or fewer employees (11 percent are at firms with 100 or fewer employees). In a small number of cases (about 6 percent) data on the number of employees were not available, so these cases are excluded from the table.

The table shows that, consistent with findings presented earlier in this report, proportional earnings losses are higher for workers at smaller firms. The average three-year proportional losses for workers at firms with 100 or fewer employees are about 28.6 percent, compared with just 17.3 percent for workers at firms with more than 7,500 employees. However, we do not find substantial differences in the average ratings for workers at smaller firms versus larger firms. It is true that individuals at smaller firms do appear to have higher ratings, but the differences are much smaller than those for proportional losses. The average final rating for workers at firms with 100 or fewer employees is 18.5, while for workers at firms with more than 7,500 employees it is 17.7. This result suggests that the correlation between ratings and losses demonstrated in Figure 5.3 and Figure 5.5 is not driven simply by a correlation between ratings and firm size.

Table B.3 also compares the distribution of back, upper-extremity, and lower-extremity injuries for different-sized firms. These three categories account for more than 75 percent of all single-injury, summary-rated claims. While looking at just these three categories is certainly not a perfect check of differences in the injury distribution, because there is heterogeneity within the upper and lower extremity categories, such an examination at least provides a sense of whether there are any broad differences in the types of injuries at firms of different sizes. In general, the percentage of lower-extremity injury cases appears to be unrelated to firm size. The percentage of back cases does appear to decline slightly from the largest firms to the smallest

Table B.3
Characteristics of Cases by Firm Size

Firm Size by Number of Employees	Final Rating	Proportional Earnings Losses	Back Injuries (% of all injuries)	Upper-Extremity Injuries (% of all injuries)	Lower-Extremity Injuries (% of all injuries)	Number of Observations
100 or fewer	18.5	28.6	35.4	20.6	18.1	7,707
101 to 500	18.1	24.1	34.6	22.1	17.8	14,434
501 to 1,500	17.4	19.4	33.0	24.2	18.7	12,946
1,501 to 2,500	16.8	16.6	33.6	25.3	18.6	6,242
2,501 to 5,000	17.1	17.1	33.4	25.6	18.6	6,751
5,001 to 7,500	17.3	16.2	30.9	28.3	17.1	3,241
More than 7,500	17.7	17.3	32.3	26.7	18.8	16,767
Total	17.7	20.3	33.4	24.4	18.4	68,088

firms, but the difference is small. The largest differences appear to involve upper-extremity injuries, which appear to be more common at larger firms (20.6 percent of cases at firms with fewer than 100 employees compared with 26.7 percent of cases at firms with more than 7,500 employees).

The increasing fraction of upper-extremity injuries might weaken the conclusions of this discussion with respect to horizontal equity if the increasing fraction were associated with what were found to be the more-overrated injury types.[7] However, consider the frequency of shoulder and elbow injuries by firm size, which are two of the most underrated and overrated injuries, respectively (see Table 5.1). Shoulder injuries are slightly more likely to be observed at larger firms; they account for about 5.9 percent of injuries at firms with 100 or fewer employees and 7 percent of injuries at firms with more than 7,500 employees. Elbow injuries are also slightly more frequent at larger firms; they account for 2.8 percent and 3.2 percent of injuries at firms in the smallest firm-size category and largest firm-size category, respectively. All of this leads us to conclude that the findings in Chapter Five are not substantially driven by a correlation between firm size and the characteristics of injuries.

---

[7] The terms "overrated" or "underrated" are not used in a pejorative sense. The terms simply refer to injury types that have average ratings that appear particularly high or particularly low relative to earnings losses.

Evaluating the Occupation Adjustments to the Disability Rating Schedule

The California disability rating schedule has a unique classification system in which each work occupation is placed into one of 44 groups based on the physical demands of the work the occupation involves and the corresponding risk of injury. For instance, a computer programmer and a stenographer would be placed into the same classification because the primary physical demands on those workers stem from repetitive typing motion. Likewise, carpenters and electricians are grouped into the same category because of the similar physical demands of their work.[1] For every occupation group, each type of disability is assigned a modifier to the disability ratings (i.e., an *occupation adjustment*) based on whether that disability is expected to have a greater or lesser effect on an individual's ability to compete in the labor market.

The occupation adjustments are a key feature of the California rating schedule's attempt to move from a measure of functional impairment to a measure of disability. However, the occupation adjustments are not based on an empirical analysis of how different impairments disable individuals in different types of work. In some cases, the disabling effects of two different impairments for workers in two different occupations would seem to be straightforward—a back impairment is very likely to be more disabling than a hearing impairment for a manual laborer, whereas the reverse is almost certainly true for a piano tuner. In other examples, it is far more difficult to determine the likely relationship between an impairment and the level of disability for a workers in different professions. Would a carpenter be more disabled than an electrician, or vice versa, from a back impairment, a shoulder impairment, or a hip impairment?

We do not provide a comprehensive review of how various kinds of impairments affect an individual's ability to work in certain occupations. Such an analysis would be valuable, but it is difficult to accomplish given the data we have available, for two reasons. First, despite the large amount of our data, for most occupation-

---

[1] Occupations are not grouped by the level of physical risk involved in the work or the types of injuries that a worker in that occupation might suffer; instead, the classification is based on physical demands, because those are the factors that, in theory, will make certain impairments more or less damaging to an individual's ability to work.

injury pairs there would simply not be enough observations to perform a reliable analysis. Second, the occupation groups in our data are not the same ones used in the current California disability rating schedule. The occupation groups used in the California schedule were changed as of April 1, 1997, the cutoff date for our data. The occupation groups were updated to include some newer occupations and to eliminate some older ones, and the actual modifiers themselves were rearranged in an attempt to better capture the impact of different impairments on an individual's ability to work in different jobs.

Because of these limitations, we provide a simpler evaluation of the occupation adjustments. We categorize cases into one of three groups—those with a positive occupation adjustment, those with a negative occupation adjustment, and those with a zero occupation adjustment—and ask whether we actually observe higher earnings losses in cases in which the adjustment is positive (i.e., the disability rating is raised for a particular occupation-impairment pair) and lower earnings losses in cases in which the adjustment is negative (i.e., the disability rating is reduced for a particular occupation-impairment pair). This analysis is done using the pre-1997 adjustments. We then match a sample of our data to the new occupation adjustments and perform a similar analysis to see how well the post–April 1, 1997 adjustments perform.

We begin by considering a sample of all single-disability, summary-rated claims for which we have information on the pre-1997 occupation adjustments—a sample of 71,796 claims. Of those claims, 25,993 received no adjustment for their occupation-impairment pairs, 35,855 received a positive adjustment, and 9,948 received a negative adjustment. For our analysis, we broke down the sample into groups by disability rating—1 to 5 percent, 6 to 10 percent, and on up to a rating of 30 percent—and then grouped together all the observations with a rating of 31 percent or higher (see Figure C.1). We then calculated proportional earnings losses for each occupation adjustment category by rating group.

The notion behind occupation adjustments is that higher ratings should be assigned to occupation-impairment pairs that will produce worse observed labor market outcomes. Therefore, if the California ratings schedule were performing well, we would expect that the earnings losses for the positive adjustments would be higher than the losses for the cases with no adjustment, while the losses for the cases with negative adjustments would be lower. If this were true, for each disability rating group in Figure C.1, the light gray bar would be the highest, the dark gray bar would be in the middle, and the black bar would be the lowest.

The results shown in the figure are striking. First, it appears that the negative adjustments perform quite well, in that occupation-impairment pairs with a negative adjustment experience considerably lower earnings losses. The results might even suggest that a larger downward adjustment would be appropriate. On the other hand, Figure C.1 provides no evidence that the cases with positive adjustments

Figure C.1
Three-Year Earnings Losses by Occupation Adjustment and Disability Rating

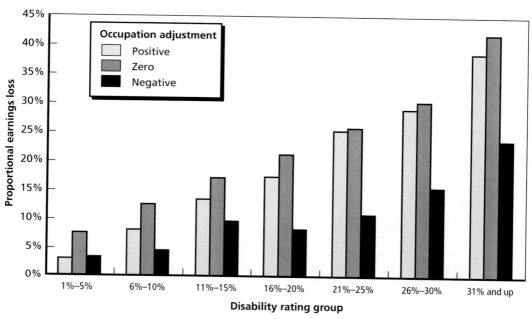

experience higher earnings losses. In fact, for every rating group, the observed losses for the no-adjustment (zero) cases are higher than those for the positive adjustment cases, although in many cases the differences are small. Note that while this analysis is based on a sample of all impairment types pooled together, we get the same results when we consider back injuries, knee injuries, shoulder injuries, and loss of grasping power injuries separately.

While this analysis casts some doubt on the effectiveness of the occupation adjustments, its utility is limited given the fact that it is based on the old California ratings system. Unfortunately, there is no crosswalk to match the occupations in our sample to the occupations in the new system. We were able to match some of the observations in our sample to the new occupation groups using text descriptions of the injured workers' jobs that were contained in the DEU database.

Table C.1 displays the standard ratings and old and new occupation adjustments for a sample of summary-rated, single-disability back injury claims. Of the 23,894 total observations, for which we had information on the old occupation adjustments, we were able to match 7,010 (approximately 29 percent) to the new occupation codes. The table lists the occupation adjustments for both the full sample and the matched sample broken down by positive, zero, and negative adjustments. One can see that the average standard ratings are very close for all the samples, which is

Table C.1
Average Standard Ratings by Occupation Adjustment Using the Old and New Adjustment System (Summary-Rated, Single-Disability Back Injury Claim)

		Old Adjustments: Full Sample	Old Adjustments: Matched Sample	New Adjustments
Positive adjustment	Standard rating	19.99	19.89	20.07
		(0.21)	(0.46)	(0.37)
	N	4,484	895	1,462
No adjustment	Standard rating	20.36	19.90	18.93
		(0.14)	(0.26)	(0.33)
	N	10,431	2,987	1,584
Negative adjustment	Standard rating	20.23	19.39	19.77
		(0.14)	(0.24)	(0.22)
	N	8,979	3,128	3,964

NOTE: Standard errors appear in parentheses. N = number of observations in sample.

important because it means that any differences in earnings losses we observe among the groups will not be driven by unobserved differences in injury severity. Additionally our matched sample is reasonably close to the full sample, at least in terms of injury severity.

Looking at the sample sizes in each of the groups can provide some insight into the effect of the 1997 reforms. By comparing the old adjustments in the full sample with those in the matched sample, we can see that the matched sample contains relatively fewer positive adjustments and relatively more negative adjustments. It is hard to say why this is so, other than it may be a random outcome of matching on the text descriptions. A more interesting comparison is between the old adjustments in the matched sample and new adjustments. In the matched sample, 43 percent of the cases receive no adjustment under the old system (i.e., the 2,987 observations with no adjustments represent 43 percent of the total number of matched observations), whereas just 23 percent of cases receive no adjustment under the new system. This change seems slightly skewed toward more negative adjustments, with the portion of positive adjustments rising from 13 percent to 21 percent and the portion of negative adjustments rising from 45 percent to 57 percent. Thus, the end result of the reforms seems to be a general shift away from the middle, with more cases being adjusted in either direction.

We now consider the earnings losses under the old and new system of adjustments. In Table C.2, we list the three-year proportional earnings losses for the cases in the full sample and matched sample broken down by positive, zero, and negative adjustments. In addition, we also report the estimated average total PPD benefits that the injured workers would qualify for given the final rating. We estimate the benefits by taking the final rating and applying it to the AB-749 benefit schedule,

Table C.2
Three-Year Wage Losses and Estimated PPD Benefits by Occupation Adjustment

		Old Adjustments: Full Sample	Old Adjustments: Matched Sample
Positive adjustment	Proportional losses	0.165 (0.013)	0.173 (0.011)
	Estimated PPD benefits	$24,250	$27,563
No adjustment	Proportional losses	0.194 (0.013)	0.171 (0.019)
	Estimated PPD benefits	$19,909	$22,817
Negative adjustment	Proportional losses	0.046 (0.027)	0.104 (0.020)
	Estimated PPD benefits	$14,278	$20,788

NOTE: Standard errors are shown in parentheses. Benefits are estimated assuming that workers earn enough to qualify for the 2006 benefit maximum of $230 per week.

which will be fully implemented in 2006. We assume that the workers earn enough to qualify for the maximum weekly benefit of $230 per week if the disability rating is below 70, and $270 per week if the disability rating is 70 or above. In truth, workers receive two-thirds of their weekly wage subject to the cap, but we feel it is appropriate to use the maximum, because weekly wage is missing for some of the claims in our data, and when weekly wage is not missing from claims data, more than 60 percent of injured workers receive the maximum (a figure that would likely climb to more than 90 percent if we adjusted the wage data for inflation).

We can see from Table C.2 that the old occupational adjustments functioned just as we would have expected after looking at Figure C.1. The proportional earnings losses for the cases with no adjustment are 19.4 percent on average, which are higher than the losses for cases with a positive adjustment (16.5 percent). The proportional earnings losses for the cases with a negative adjustment are extremely low, averaging just 4.6 percent. The new adjustments, represented by the numbers in the "Old Adjustments: Matched Sample" column, seem to narrow the differences between the categories somewhat. The average losses for the no-adjustment cases fall from 19.4 percent to 17.1 percent, while for the negative-adjustment cases they rise from 4.6 percent to 10.4 percent. The losses for the positive adjustment cases are slightly higher than for the no-adjustment cases in the matched sample, 17.3 percent versus 17.1 percent, but the difference between the two is not statistically different from zero.

These results suggest that the 1997 reforms improved the overall performance of the occupation adjustments. Clearly, there were many occupation-impairment pairs that had low overall earnings losses that now receive a negative adjustment, compared with a positive or zero adjustment in the old system. Likewise, the earnings losses for the positive-adjustment cases seem to have moved in the right direction, although the size of the change (from 0.165 to 0.173) appears to have been small. Note that while this analysis has been done for back injuries only, we see no reason why the results would differ if we were able to match the complete sample to the new occupation adjustments.

Despite the improvements that were made in 1997, when we compare the estimated PPD benefits for the different groups, it appears that further changes are needed. We see that while the proportional losses for the positive-adjustment cases are only 1 percent higher than those for the no-adjustment cases, the estimated PPD benefits are 21 percent higher. On the other hand, the proportional losses for the negative-adjustment cases are 39 percent lower than those for the no-adjustment cases, but the PPD benefits are just 9 percent lower. From this analysis, it seems that more work needs to be done to determine the impact of various impairments on the ability of individuals to perform certain kinds of work.

Further Analysis of Consistency in Disability Ratings

In Chapter Seven, we examined inconsistency in disability ratings that results from inconsistencies in the evaluation of the same impairment by different physicians. There are two primary sources of these inconsistencies: inconsistencies in the way physicians describe the nature of a bodily impairment and inconsistencies in the reported severity of impairment. The analysis in Chapter Seven focused primarily on inconsistencies in reported severity; here, we provide some additional information on inconsistencies in the description of the type of impairment.

Table D.1 illustrates the likelihood that applicant and defense physicians "agree" on the nature of impairment by type of impairment. Note that physician agreement is slightly misleading—raters assign a specific disability category based on physicians' reports, so it is certainly possible that two physicians could totally agree on the nature of an impairment and still provide reports that lead to two different disability categories for that impairment.

The "All Cases" column in the table illustrates the percentage of cases in which the defense rating (we use "rating" to represent both the actual percent rating *and* the classification of impairment type that results from a given physician's medical report) has the same disability category *and* the same number of claimed impairments, which we classify as cases agreeing on type. Thus, if the applicant rating indicates a single back impairment, whereas the defense rating claims a back impairment and a shoulder impairment, then the case would not be considered "in agreement." The right-hand column in Table D.1 considers only those cases in which the applicant and defense ratings indicate the same number of impairments and presents the percentage of cases in which there is agreement on the specific type(s) of impairment(s). For each impairment type listed in the table, the fraction of cases in the right-hand column must be at least as high as that in the middle column (because the right-hand column excludes cases in which the applicant and defense ratings indicate a different number of impairments, and hence, automatically count as not being in agreement); in fact, the fraction of cases is higher for every impairment type.

The extent of disagreement over type of impairment is surprising. Even when physicians agree on the number of impairments, they often disagree on the specific type of impairment. For loss of grasping power, the fraction of cases indicating agreement is just 39 percent, even when the physicians agree that it is a single-impairment case. This might be because there are a number of reasonably close impairment substitutes for loss of grasping power in the California system. For instance, it may be difficult, particularly for a rater reading a medical report, to distinguish loss of grasping power from an impairment in all five digits on one hand. Nonetheless, such a distinction does matter in terms of the standard rating an injured worker receives.

Table D.1
Percentage of Cases in Which the Defense Agrees with the Applicant on the Type and Number of Impairments Claimed

Type of Impairment Claimed by Applicant	All Cases	Cases in Which Defense Agrees on Number of Impairments
Single Impairment		
General lower-extremity impairment	64%	71%
Knee impairment	86%	94%
Ankle impairment	82%	87%
Impaired hearing	85%	94%
Impaired finger: Four digits	45%	51%
Impaired finger: Five digits	47%	51%
Loss of grasping power	35%	39%
General upper-extremity impairment	54%	61%
Shoulder impairment	69%	78%
Elbow impairment	57%	64%
Wrist impairment	61%	66%
Back impairment	81%	93%
Psychiatric impairment	49%	63%
Multiple Impairments		
Loss of grasping power and back impairment	21%	39%
General upper-extremity and back injuries	32%	64%
Shoulder and back injuries	38%	74%
Wrist and back injuries	27%	53%
General lower-extremity and back injuries	35%	66%
Knee and back injuries	47%	90%
Ankle and back injuries	36%	77%
Psychiatric impairment and back impairment	33%	77%
PTHS and back injuries	21%	66%

Bibliography

American Medical Association, *Guides to the Evaluation of Permanent Impairment,* 5th ed., Chicago: AMA, 2000.

Barth, Peter S., and Michael Niss, *Permanent Partial Disability Benefits: Interstate Differences,* Cambridge, Mass.: Workers Compensation Research Institute, 1999.

Bellusci, Dave, WCIRB chief actuary, testimony before the California Senate Industrial Relations Committee, Sacramento, Calif., November 25, 2003.

Berkowitz, Monroe, "Workers' Compensation Agencies Websites," *Workers' Compensation Policy Review*, Vol. 1, No. 2, March/April, 2001, pp. 21–27.

Berkowitz, Monroe, and John F. Burton, Jr., *Permanent Disability Benefits in Workers' Compensation*, Kalamazoo, Mich.: W.E. Upjohn Institute for Employment Research, 1987.

Berkowitz, Monroe, and Guy Pascale, "Grading the Annual Reports of Workers' Compensation Agencies: Round Two," in John F. Burton, Jr., and Timothy P. Schmidle, eds., *1996 Workers' Compensation Year Book*, Horsham, Pa.: LRP Publications, 1995, pp. I-148–I-153.

Biddle, Jeffrey, *Estimation and Analysis of Long-Term Wage Losses and Wage Replacement Rates of Washington State Workers' Compensation Claimants,* Olympia, Wash.: Department of Labor and Industry, 1998.

Blundell, Richard, and Thomas MaCurdy, "Labor Supply: A Review of Alternative Approaches," in Orley Ashenfelter and David Card, eds., *Handbook of Labor Economics,* Vol. 3, Amsterdam, The Netherlands: Elsevier Science, 1999, pp. 1559–1695.

Boden, Leslie I., *The AMA Guides in Maryland: An Assessment,* Cambridge, Mass.: Workers' Compensation Research Institute, 1992.

Boden, Leslie I., and Monica Galizzi, "Economic Consequences of Workplace Injuries and Illnesses: Lost Earnings and Benefit Adequacy," *American Journal of Industrial Medicine,* Vol. 36, No. 5, 1999, pp. 487–503.

Boden, Leslie I., Robert T. Reville, and Jeff Biddle, "The Adequacy of Workers' Compensation Cash Benefits," in Karen Roberts, John F. Burton, Jr., and Matt Bodah, eds., *Workplace Injuries and Diseases: Prevention and Compensation: Essays in Honor of Terry Thomason,* Kalamazoo, Mich.: W.E. Upjohn Institute for Employment Research, 2005.

133

Bureau of National Affairs, *BNA's Workers' Compensation Report*, BNA, June 14, 1996.

Burton, John F., Jr., "Compensation for Permanent Partial Disability," in John D. Worrall, ed., *Safety and the Work Force: Incentives and Disincentives for Workers' Compensation*, Ithaca, N.Y.: ILR Press, 1983, pp. 18–60.

Burton, John F., Jr., "Editor's Comments on Permanent Partial Disability Benefits: A Multi-Jurisdictional Inventory of Benefit Structures," in John F. Burton, Jr., and Timothy P. Schmidle, eds., *1996 Workers' Compensation Year Book*, Horsham, Pa.: LRP Publications, 1995, pp. I-59–I-60.

Burton, John F., Jr., "Permanent Partial Disability Benefits: The Criteria for Evaluation," *Workers' Compensation Monitor*, Vol. 10, No. 4, July/August, 1997, pp. 10–31.

Burton, John F., Jr., "Permanent Partial Disability Benefits: A Reexamination," *Workers' Compensation Monitor*, Vol. 9, No. 4, July/August, 1996, pp. 1–15.

Burton, John F., Jr., and James R. Chelius, "Workplace Safety and Health Regulations: Rationale and Results," in Bruce E. Kaufman, ed., *Government Regulation of the Employment Relationship*, Madison, Wis.: Industrial Relations Research Association, 1997.

Burton, John F., Jr., and Timothy P. Schmidle, *1995 Workers' Compensation Year Book*, Horsham, Pa.: LRP Publications, 1994.

Burton, John F., Jr., and Timothy P. Schmidle, *1996 Workers' Compensation Year Book*, Horsham, Pa.: LRP Publications, 1995.

Burton, John F., Jr., and Timothy P. Schmidle, "Workers' Compensation Insurance Rates: National Averages Up, Interstate Differences Widen," in John F. Burton, Jr., and Timothy P. Schmidle, eds., *Workers' Compensation Desk Book*, Horsham, Pa.: LRP Publications, 1992, pp. I-6–I-25.

Butler, Richard, "Safety Incentives in Workers' Compensation," in John F. Burton, Jr., and Timothy P. Schmidle, eds., *1995 Workers' Compensation Year Book*, Horsham, Pa.: LRP Publications, 1994, pp. I-82–I-91.

California Senate Interim Committee, *Report to the Senate on Workmen's Compensation Benefits*, 1953.

California Workers' Compensation Insurance Rating Bureau, *WCIRB Bulletin No. 2003-16*, San Francisco: WCIRB, 2003a.

Chelius, James R., and John F. Burton, Jr., "Who Actually Pays for Workers' Compensation?" *Workers' Compensation Monitor*, Vol. 5, No. 6, November/December, 1992, pp. 25–35.

Chelius, James R., and John F. Burton, Jr., "Who Actually Pays for Workers' Compensation? The Empirical Evidence," *Workers' Compensation Monitor*, Vol. 7, No. 6, November/December 1994, pp. 20–27.

Dehejia, Rajeev H., and Sadek Wahba, "Causal Effects in Non-Experimental Studies: Re-Evaluating the Evaluation of Training Programs," *Journal of the American Statistical Association*, Vol. 94, 1999, pp. 1053–1062.

Division of Workers' Compensation (California), *Schedule for Rating Permanent Disabilities,* California Department of Industrial Relations, 1997.

Durbin, David, and Richard J. Butler, "Prevention of Disability from Work-Related Sources: The Roles of Risk Management, Government Interventions, and Insurance," in Terry Thomason, John F. Burton, Jr., and Douglas E. Hyatt, eds., *New Approaches to Disability in the Workplace,* Madison, Wis.: Industrial Relations Research Association, 1998, pp. 63–86.

Flor, Herta, and D. C. Turk, "Etiological Theories and Treatments for Chronic Back Pain: I. Somatic Models and Interventions," *Pain,* Vol. 19, 1984, pp. 105–121.

Hallmark, Shelby, *State Workers' Compensation Laws, January 2003,* Washington, D.C.: Office of Workers' Compensation Programs, Employment Standards Administration, U.S. Department of Labor, 2003.

Hannigan, Dennis J., and Charles Lawrence Swezey, *California Workers' Compensation Practice,* 4th ed., Oakland, Calif.: Continuing Education of the Bar—California, 2003.

Heckman, James J., "What Has Been Learned about Labor Supply in the Past Twenty Years?" *American Economic Review,* Vol. 83, No. 2, May 1993, pp. 116–121.

Heckman, James J., and V. Joseph Hotz, "Choosing Among Alternative Non-Experimental Methods for Estimating the Impact of Social Programs: The Case of Manpower Training," *Journal of the American Statistical Association,* Vol. 84, 1989, pp. 862–874.

Holland, Paul W., "Statistics and Causal Inference," *Journal of the American Statistical Association,* Vol. 81, 1986, pp. 945–970.

Hunt, H. Allan, ed., *Adequacy of Earnings Replacement in Workers' Compensation Programs: A Report of the Study Panel on Benefit Adequacy of the Workers' Compensation Steering Committee,* National Academy of Social Insurance, Kalamazoo, Mich.: W.E. Upjohn Institute for Employment Research, 2004.

Imbens, Guido W., Donald Rubin, and Bruce Sacerdote, "Estimating the Effect of Unearned Income on Labor Earnings, Savings, and Consumption: Evidence from a Survey of Lottery Players," *American Economic Review,* Vol. 91, No. 4, September 2001, pp. 778–794.

Industrial Medical Council, *Guidelines for Evaluation of Neuromusculoskeletal Evaluation Disability,* Department of Industrial Relations, State of California, 2003.

Industrial Medical Council, *Physician's Guide to Medical Practice in the California Workers' Compensation System,* 3rd ed., Department of Industrial Relations, State of California, 2001.

Institute of Medicine, Committee on Pain, Disability, and Chronic Illness Behavior, *Pain and Disability: Clinical, Behavioral, and Public Policy Perspectives,* Washington, D.C.: National Academy Press, 1987.

Joulfaian, David, and Mark Wilhelm, "Inheritances and Labor Supply," *Journal of Human Resources,* Vol. 29, No. 4, 1994, 1205–1234.

Killingsworth, Mark R., and James J. Heckman, "Female Labor Supply: A Survey," in Orley Ashenfelter and Richard Layard, eds., *Handbook of Labor Economics,* Vol. 1, Amsterdam, The Netherlands: Elsevier Science, 1986, pp. 103–204.

Lalonde, Robert, "Evaluating the Econometric Evaluations of Training Programs," *American Economic Review,* Vol. 76, 1986, pp. 604–620.

Leigh, J. Paul, Steven Markowitz, Marianne Fahs, and Philip Landrigan, *Costs of Occupational Injuries and Illnesses,* Ann Arbor, Mich.: The University of Michigan Press, 2000.

Melzack, R., "From the Gate to the Neuromatrix," *Pain,* Supp. 6, 1999a, pp. S121–S126.

Melzack, R., "Pain—An Overview," *Acta Anaesthesiologica Scandinavica,* Vol. 43, 1999b, pp. 880–884.

Melzack, R., and P. D. Wall, "Pain Mechanisms: A New Theory," *Science,* Vol. 150, 1965, pp. 971–979.

Merskey, H., "Association for the Study of Pain, Subcommittee on Taxonomy: Chronic Pain Syndromes and Definition of Pain Terms," *Pain,* Supp. 3, 1986, p. S1.

Moore, Michael, and W. Kip Viscusi, *Compensation Mechanisms for Job Risks,* Princeton, N.J.: Princeton University Press, 1990.

National Academy of Social Insurance, *Adequacy of Earnings Replacement in Workers' Compensation Programs,* Kalamazoo, Mich.: W.E. Upjohn Institute for Employment Research, 2004.

National Commission on State Workmen's Compensation Laws, *The Report of the National Commission on State Workmen's Compensation Laws,* Washington, D.C.: Government Printing Office, 1972.

National Council on Compensation Insurance (NCCI), *Permanent Partial Disability Benefits: A Multi-Jurisdiction Inventory of Benefit Structures,* Boca Raton, Fla.: NCCI, 1995.

Pace, Nicholas, et al., *Improving Dispute Resolution for California's Injured Workers,* Santa Monica, Calif.: RAND Corporation, MR-1425-ICJ, 2003.

Park, Yong-Seung, and Richard J. Butler, "Permanent Partial Disability Awards and Wage Loss," *Journal of Risk and Insurance,* Vol. 67, No. 3, 2000, pp. 331–349.

Pencavel, John, "Labor Supply of Men: A Survey," in Orley Ashenfelter and Richard Layard, eds., *Handbook of Labor Economics,* Vol. 1, Amsterdam, The Netherlands: Elsevier Science, 1986, pp. 3–102.

Peterson, Mark A., Robert T. Reville, Rachel Kaganoff Stern, and Peter S. Barth, *Compensating Permanent Workplace Injuries: A Study of California's System,* Santa Monica, Calif.: RAND Corporation, MR-920-ICJ, 1997.

Reinke, Derek, and Mike Manley, *2002 Oregon Workers' Compensation Premium Rate Ranking,* Research and Analysis Section, Salem, Ore.: Oregon Department of Consumer and Business Services, January 2003.

Reville, Robert T., "The Impact of a Disabling Workplace Injury on Earnings and Labor Force Participation," in John Haltiwanger and Julia Lane, eds., *Contributions to Economic*

Analysis, Amsterdam, London, and New York: Elsevier Science, North-Holland, 1999, pp. 147–173.

Reville, Robert T., Jayanta Bhattacharya, and Lauren Sager, "New Methods and Data Sources for Measuring the Economic Consequences of Workplace Injuries," *American Journal of Industrial Medicine*, Vol. 40, 2001a, pp. 452–463.

Reville, Robert T., Leslie I. Boden, Jeff E. Biddle, and Christopher Mardesich, *An Evaluation of New Mexico Workers' Compensation Permanent Partial Disability and Return to Work*, Santa Monica, Calif.: RAND Corporation, MR-1414-ICJ, 2001b.

Reville, Robert T., Frank W. Neuhauser, Jayanta Bhattacharya, and Craig Martin, "Comparing Severity of Impairment for Different Permanent Upper Extremity Musculoskeletal Injuries," *Journal of Occupational Rehabilitation*, Vol. 12, No. 3, 2002a, pp. 205–222.

Reville, Robert T., Suzanne Polich, Seth Seabury, and Elizabeth Giddens, *Permanent Disability at Private, Self-Insured Firms: A Study of Earnings Loss, Replacement, and Return to Work for Workers' Compensation Claimants*, Santa Monica, Calif.: RAND Corporation, MR-1268-ICJ, 2001c.

Reville, Robert T., and Robert F. Schoeni, *Disability from Injuries at Work: The Effects on Earnings and Employment*, Santa Monica, Calif.: RAND Corporation, DRU-2554, 2001.

Reville, Robert T., Robert Schoeni, and Craig W. Martin, *Trends in Earnings Loss from Disabling Workplace Injuries in California: The Role of Economic Conditions*, Santa Monica, Calif.: RAND Corporation, MR-1457-ICJ, 2002b.

Reville, Robert T., Seth A. Seabury, and Frank Neuhauser, *Evaluation of California's Permanent Disability Rating Schedule: Interim Report*, Santa Monica, Calif.: RAND Corporation, DB-443-ICJ, 2003.

Roy-Byrne, Peter, et al., "Evidence for Limited Validity of the Revised Global Assessment of Functioning Scale," *Psychiatric Services*, Vol. 47, 1996, pp. 864–866.

Royal Commission of Workers' Compensation in British Columbia, *Final Report*, Vancouver, B.C.: Royal Commission, 1999.

Sinclair, Sandra, and John F. Burton, Jr., "Development of a Schedule for Compensation of Noneconomic Loss: Quality-of-Life Values vs. Clinical Impairment Ratings," in Terry Thomason and Richard P. Chaykowski, eds., *Research in Canadian Workers' Compensation*, Kingston, Ontario: IRC Press, 1995.

Spieler, Emily A., Peter S. Barth, John F. Burton, Jr., Jay Himmelstein, and Linda Rudolph, "Recommendations to Guide Revision of the Guides to the Evaluation of Permanent Impairment," *Journal of the American Medical Association*, Vol. 283, No. 4, January 26, 2000, pp. 519–523.

Swezey, Charles Lawrence, "Permanent Disability," in Dennis J. Hannigan and Charles Lawrence Swezey, *California Workers' Compensation Practice*, 4th ed., Oakland, Calif.: Continuing Education of the Bar—California, 2003, pp. 251–321.

Thomason, Terry, "Economic Incentives and Workplace Safety," in Terrence Sullivan and John Frank, eds., *Preventing and Managing Disabling Injury at Work*, London and New York: Taylor & Francis, 2003, pp. 183–203.

Thomason, Terry, and John F. Burton, Jr., "Economic Effects of Workers' Compensation in the United States: Private Insurance and the Administration of Compensation Claims," *Journal of Labor Economics*, Vol. 11, No. 1, Part 2, January 1993, pp. S1–S37.

Thomason, Terry, Timothy P. Schmidle, and John F. Burton, Jr., *Workers' Compensation: Benefits, Costs, and Safety Under Alternative Insurance Arrangements*, Kalamazoo, Mich.: W.E. Upjohn Institute for Employment Research, 2001.

Thurber, Packard, ed., *Evaluation of Industrial Disability*, 2nd ed., New York: Oxford University Press, 1960.

Turk, Dennis C., and Herta Flor, "Etiological Theories and Treatments for Chronic Back Pain: II. Psychological Models and Interventions," *Pain*, Vol. 19, 1984, pp. 209–233.

Turk, Dennis C., and Ronald M. Melzack, *Handbook of Pain Assessment*, New York, N.Y.: Guilford Press, 1992.

U.S. Chamber of Commerce, *2003 Analysis of Workers' Compensation Laws*, Washington, D.C.: U.S. Chamber of Commerce, 2003.

Welch, Eli P., "Permanent Disability Evaluation," in Melvin S. Witt, ed., *California Workmen's Compensation Practice*, Berkeley, Calif.: California Continuing Education of the Bar, 1973, pp. 531–571.

Welch, Eli P., "Presentation of Permanent Disability Ratings," presented to the California Workers' Compensation Study Commission, 1964.

Williams, Cecili Thompson, Virginia P. Reno, and John F. Burton, Jr., *Workers' Compensation: Benefits, Coverage, and Costs, 2001*, Washington, D.C.: National Academy of Social Insurance, 2003.

Work Loss Data Institute (WLDI), *State Report Cards for Workers' Comp*, Corpus Christi, Tex.: WLDI, February 2003.

Wynn, Barbara, *Adopting Medicare Fee Schedules: Considerations for the California Workers' Compensation Program*, Santa Monica, Calif.: RAND Corporation, MR-1776-ICJ, 2003.